STUDIES IN THE BOOK
OF LAMEN...

Travis

STUDIES IN BIBLICAL THEOLOGY

STUDIES IN THE BOOK OF LAMENTATIONS

NORMAN K. GOTTWALD

Columbia University

SCM PRESS LTD
56 BLOOMSBURY STREET
LONDON

First published 1954

Printed in Great Britain by
Robert Cunningham and Sons Ltd.
Longbank Works, Alva

CONTENTS

TRANSLATION OF THE BOOK OF LAMENTATIONS

1. *Aleph*
   O how
   The city dwells alone, once great with people!
   She has become as a widow, once great among the nations!
   Princess over the cities, she has become tributary.

2. *Beth*
   Bitterly she weeps in the night, her tears upon her cheeks;
   There is none to comfort her among all her lovers;
   All her friends have betrayed her; they have become her
      enemies.

3. *Gimel*
   Judah has gone into exile because of affliction and harsh servi-
      tude;
   She dwells among the nations, she finds no rest;
   All her pursuers overtake her amidst the narrow defiles.

4. *Daleth*
   The ways of Zion mourn because none go to the festival;
   All her gates are desolate, her priests groan;
   Her maidens are driven away, and she herself is bitter.

5. *He*
   Her enemies have gained the ascendancy, her foes have
      triumphed,
   For Yahweh has afflicted her because of the multitude of her
      sins;
   Her children go into captivity before the enemy.

6. *Waw*
   Vanished from the daughter of Zion is all her glory;
   Her princes have become as stags, they find no pasture;
   And they flee without strength before the pursuer.

7. *Zayin*
   Jerusalem remembers in the days of her affliction and wandering
   All her pleasant things that she had from days of old,
   When her people fell into the hand of the enemy, and there was
      none to help her.
   The enemies see her, they laugh at her annihilation.

8. *Heth*
Jerusalem has greatly sinned, therefore she has become filthy;
All her admirers despise her, for they behold her nakedness;
Even she herself groans and turns away.

9. *Teth*
Her defilement is in her skirts; she does not consider her doom,
So that her fall is awesome, with none to comfort her.
Behold, O Yahweh, my affliction, for the enemy magnifies
    himself!

10. *Yodh*
The enemy stretched forth his hand upon all her precious things;
For she has seen nations enter her sanctuary,
Those whom thou didst forbid to enter thy assembly!

11. *Kaph*
All her people groan seeking bread;
They exchange their valuables for food to restore life.
Behold, O Yahweh and consider, for I am despised!

12. *Lamedh*
Is it nothing to you, all you who pass by? Behold and consider
If there is any pain like my pain which was dealt to me,
Which Yahweh inflicted in the day of his fierce anger.

13. *Mem*
From on high he cast fire, it penetrated my bones;
He spread a snare for my feet, he turned me back;
He made me desolate, faint all the day.

14. *Nun*
My sins are bound together as a yoke; in his hands they are
    entwined;
They ascend upon my neck; he causes my strength to fail;
The Lord gave me into the hands of those whom I cannot
    withstand.

15. *Samekh*
He has made light of all my mighty ones, the Lord in my midst;
He has called a festival against me to shatter my young men;
The Lord has trodden the winepress of the virgin daughter of
    Judah.

16. *Ayin*
Because of these things I weep, my eyes flow with tears;
For a comforter is denied me, one to revive my courage;
My sons are desolate, for the enemy is mighty.

17. *Pe*
Zion stretches forth her hands; she has no comforters;
Yahweh has decreed for Jacob that his neighbours should be
his enemies;
Jerusalem has become filthy among them.

18. *Sadhe*
Yahweh—righteous is he, for I have rebelled against his com-
mand!
Hear now all peoples, and behold my pain!
My daughters and young men go into captivity.

19. *Qoph*
I cry out to my lovers, they betray me;
My priests and elders perish in the city,
For they seek food for themselves to restore their life.

20. *Resh*
Behold, O Yahweh, for I am distressed, my emotions are in
tumult!
My heart is faint within me, for I have been very rebellious!
In the street the sword slays, in the house it is as death.

21. *Šin*
Listen when I groan, there is none to comfort me!
All my enemies rejoice over my fate, that thou hast done it;
Bring to pass the day thou didst proclaim when they shall be
as I!

22. *Taw*
Bring all their evil before thee! And do with them
As thou hast done with me, because of all my sins!
For great are my groanings and my heart is faint.

CHAPTER TWO

1. *Aleph*
O how
The Lord has eclipsed in his anger the daughter of Zion!
Has cast from heaven to earth the glory of Israel!
And has taken no thought of his footstool in the day of his
anger!

2. *Beth*
The Lord has destroyed without mercy all the pastures of Jacob;
He has pulled down in his anger the fortifications of the
daughter of Judah;
He has brought down to the ground in dishonour her king and
priests.

3. *Gimel*
   He has cut off in fierce anger all the strength of Israel;
   He has turned back their right hand from before the enemy,
   And has burned in Jacob as a fire, a flame consuming round
      about.

4. *Daleth*
   He has bent the bow as an enemy, his hand was firmly set;
   He has slain as a foe all the delightful things of the eye;
   In the tent of the daughter of Zion he has poured out his wrath
      like fire.

5. *He*
   The Lord has become like an enemy, he has destroyed Israel;
   He has destroyed all her palaces, he has ruined all his forti-
      fications,
   And multiplied in the daughter of Judah mourning and
      moaning.

6. *Waw*
   He has broken down his tabernacle like a garden hut, he has
      ruined his place of abode;
   Yahweh has caused to be forgotten in Zion festival and Sabbath,
   And spurned in the indignation of his anger king and priest.

7. *Zayin*
   The Lord has spurned his altar, he has abhorred his sanctuary;
   He has delivered into the hand of the enemy the walls of her
      palaces;
   Clamour was raised in the house of Yahweh as on a day of
      festival.

8. *Heth*
   Yahweh determined to destroy the wall of the daughter of Zion;
   He stretched forth the measuring line, he withheld not his hand
      from destruction;
   And he caused rampart and wall to mourn, together they
      languish.

9. *Teth*
   Her gates have sunk into the earth, he has shattered her bars;
   Her king and princes are among the nations, there is no torah;
   Even her prophets receive no vision from the Lord.

10. *Yodh*
    The elders of the daughter of Zion sit silently on the ground;
    They cast dust on their heads and put on sackcloth;
    The maidens of Jerusalem bow their heads to the ground.

11. *Kaph*

My eyes are spent with tears, my emotions are in tumult;
My heart is poured out in grief because of the destruction of
    my people,
Because child and suckling faint in the city's open places.

12. *Lamedh*

To their mothers they say, 'Where is bread?' and there is none,
As they faint like those wounded in the city's open places,
As their life is poured out on the bosom of their mothers.

13. *Mem*

How shall I uphold you, with what shall I compare you, O
    daughter of Jerusalem?
To what shall I liken you, and how comfort you, virgin daughter
    of Zion?
For great as the sea is your ruin; who can heal you?

14. *Nun*

Your prophets envisioned for you emptiness and falsehood;
They did not disclose your iniquity in order to prevent your
    captivity,
But they envisioned for you oracles of emptiness and seduction.

15. *Samekh*

All who pass by clap their hands at you;
They hiss and shake their heads at the daughter of Jerusalem;
" Is this the city of which they said, 'perfect in beauty, the joy
    of all the earth'? "

16. *Pe*

All your enemies open their mouth at you;
They hiss and gnash their teeth, they say 'We have destroyed
    her!'
'Surely this is the day for which we waited! It is ours! We see
    it!'

17. *Ayin*

Yahweh has done what he purposed; he has accomplished his
    threat
Which he decreed from days of old; he has pulled down without
    mercy,
And caused the enemy to rejoice over you; he has exalted the
    strength of your enemies.

18. *Sadhe*

Cry aloud to the Lord, the Wall[1] of the daughter of Zion!
Let tears descend as a torrent day and night!
Allow yourself no relief, cease not weeping!

---

[1] חוֹמַת is understood as an apposition to אֲדֹבִי (cf. Zech. 2.5 for the
notion of Yahweh as a protective wall).

19. *Qoph*
Arise, cry out in the night, at the beginning of the nightwatches!
Pour out your heart like water in the presence of the Lord!
Lift up your hands to him for your children's lives,
Who faint in the famine at the head of every street.

20. *Resh*
Behold, O Yahweh, and consider to whom thou hast done thus!
Shall women eat the fruit of their womb, their fondled children?
Shall priest and prophet be slain in the sanctuary of the Lord?

21. *Šin*
They lie prostrate in the streets, young and old;
My maidens and young men fall by the sword;
Thou hast slain in the day of thine anger; thou hast slaughtered
without mercy.

22. *Taw*
Thou hast called as a day of festival sojourners from round
about,
And in the day of Yahweh's anger there is neither refugee nor
survivor;
Those whom I fondled and reared my enemy consumed.

CHAPTER THREE

1-3. *Aleph*
I am the man who has seen affliction by the rod of his wrath;
He has driven me and made me walk in darkness and not in
light;
Surely against me he has continually turned his hand all the day.

4-6. *Beth*
He has worn out my flesh and skin, he has shattered my bones;
He has besieged and surrounded me with bitterness and
weariness;
He has made me dwell in dark places like the primeval dead.

7-9. *Gimel*
He has walled me about so that I cannot escape; he has made
heavy my chains;
Even though I call and cry for help, he has frustrated my prayer;
He has walled up my ways with hewn stones, he has twisted
my paths.

10-12. *Daleth*
As a bear he lies in wait for me, as a lion in hiding;
He has turned me from my way and torn me, he has made me
desolate;
He bent his bow and set me as a target for the arrow.

13-15. *He*

He has driven into my heart the arrows of his quiver;
He has made me a laughing-stock to all my people, their song of derision all the day;
He has sated me with bitterness, he has saturated me with wormwood.

16-18. *Waw*

He has broken my teeth with gravel, he has made me cower in ashes;
Thou hast rejected me from peace; I have forgotten good,
So I say, 'Gone is my endurance, my hope from Yahweh.'

19-21. *Zayin*

O remember my affliction and homelessness, the wormwood and the gall!
Thou wilt surely remember and bow down to me[1];
This I take to heart, therefore I have hope.

22-24. *Heth*

The covenant loyalties of Yahweh that do not fail, his mercies that are not consumed,
Are new every morning; great is thy faithfulness!
'Yahweh is my inheritance,' says my soul, 'therefore I hope in him.'

25-27. *Teth*

Yahweh is good to him who waits for him, to the person who seeks him;
It is good that one should silently wait for the salvation of Yahweh;
It is good for a man to bear a yoke in his youth.

28-30. *Yodh*

He sits alone and is silent since it has been laid upon him;
He puts his mouth in the dust, perhaps there is hope;
He gives his cheek to the smiter, he is sated with contempt.

31-33. *Kaph*

For the Lord will not reject forever;
If he grieves, he will have mercy according to the abundance of his covenant loyalty;
For he does not afflict from his heart, nor grieve the sons of men.

---

[1] Following the Massoretic contention that the text before us has been changed to avoid the affront of God condescending to man, we have restored the original. This is one of the *tiqqune ha-sopherim*, cf. C. D. Ginsburg, *Introduction to the Massoretico-Critical Edition to the Bible* (London, 1897), pp. 347-360.

34-36. *Lamedh*

To crush under foot all the prisoners of the earth,

To turn aside a man's right in the very presence of the Most
High,

To mislead a man in his case, the Lord does not approve.

37-39. *Mem*

Who is this who speaks and it is so, unless the Lord commands?

From the mouth of the Most High has there not gone forth
evil and good?

Why should a living man murmur, a man because of his sins?

40-42. *Nun*

Let us search and examine our ways, and return to Yahweh!

Let us lift up our hearts, not our hands, to God in the
heavens!

We have sinned and rebelled; thou hast not forgiven.

43-45. *Samekh*

Thou hast clothed thyself with anger and pursued, thou hast
slain and had no mercy;

Thou hast clothed thyself in a cloud, prayer is unable to pass
through.

Offscouring and refuse thou hast made us in the midst of the
people.

46-48. *Pe*

All our enemies open their mouth at us;

Terror and pitfall have come upon us, devastation and destruction;

My eyes overflow rivers of water because of the destruction of
the daughter of my people.

49-51. *Ayin*

My eyes flow without ceasing, without respite,

Until Yahweh looks down and beholds from heaven;

What I see grieves my soul because of all the daughters of my
city.

52-54. *Sadhe*

My enemies without cause relentlessly hunt me like a bird;

They cut off my life in the pit and cast stones upon me;

Water flows over my head; I say, 'I am cut off!'

55-57. *Qoph*

I called upon thy name, O Yahweh, from the lowest pit;

Thou hast heard my voice! Do not hide thyself from my relief
and cry for help!

Thou didst draw near when I called upon thee, thou didst say,
'Fear not!'

58-60. *Resh*

O Lord, thou didst plead my cause, thou didst redeem my life;
O Yahweh, thou hast seen my oppression; judge my cause!
O Yahweh, thou hast seen all their vindictiveness, all their plans against me.

61-63. *Sin*

Thou hast heard their taunts, O Yahweh, all their plans against me,
The lips of my assailants and their thoughts against me all the day;
Behold their sitting and their rising! I am their song of derision!

64-66. *Taw*

Thou wilt recompense them, O Yahweh, according to the work of their hands;
Thou wilt give them obstinancy of heart, thy curse will be upon them;
Thou wilt pursue them in anger and destroy them from under thy heavens, O Yahweh!

CHAPTER FOUR

1. *Aleph*

O how
The gold is tarnished, the fine gold changed!
The holy stones lie scattered at the head of every street!

2. *Beth*

The precious sons of Zion, weighed against pure gold,
O how they are regarded as earthenware, the work of a potter's hand!

3. *Gimel*

Even jackals expose the breast, give suck to their whelps;
The daughter of my people has become cruel, like ostriches in the wilderness.

4. *Daleth*

The tongue of the suckling cleaves to his palate with thirst;
The children beg for bread, none is broken for them.

5. *He*

Those who ate dainties are desolate in the streets;
Those who were brought up on scarlet embrace ash heaps.

6. *Waw*

The iniquity of the daughter of my people is greater than the sin of Sodom;
She was overthrown in a moment and no hands laid upon her.

7. *Zayin*
Her princes were purer than snow, whiter than milk;
Their bodies were ruddier than corals, their form like lapis
    lazuli.

8. *Heth*
Their appearance is blacker than soot, they are not recognized
    in the streets;
Their skin shrivels on their bones, it is withered like wood.

9. *Teth*
It is better for those wounded by the sword than for those
    falling through famine,
Who languish, being stricken, for want of fruits of the field.

10. *Yodh*
The hands of compassionate women have boiled their children;
They became their food in the destruction of the daughter of
    my people.

11. *Kaph*
Yahweh has accomplished his wrath, he has poured out his
    fierce anger,
And has kindled a fire in Zion and consumed its foundations.

12. *Lamedh*
The kings of the earth did not believe, nor all the inhabitants
    of the world,
That foe or enemy could enter into the gates of Jerusalem.

13. *Mem*
It was because of the sins of her prophets, the iniquities of
    her priests,
Who shed in her midst the blood of the righteous.

14. *Nun*
Blindly they stagger in the streets, they are defiled with blood;
None are able to touch their garments.

15. *Samekh*
'Turn away! Unclean!' men say to them, 'Turn away! Turn
    away! Unclean!'
For they flee, and stagger; men say among the nations, 'They
    shall no longer sojourn.'

16. *Pe*
The face of Yahweh scattered them, he no longer considered
    them;
Men paid priests no respect, showed no favour to the elders.

17. *Ayin*
Still our eyes fail, our help is vain;
On our watchtowers we looked to a nation that could not save.

18. *Sadhe*
    They hunt our steps so that we cannot go in the open places;
    Our end draws near; our days are fulfilled, for our end has come.

19. *Qoph*
    Our pursuers were swifter than the eagles of the heavens;
    Upon the mountains they chased us, in the wilderness they
    ambushed us.

20. *Resh*
    The breath of our nostrils, the anointed of Yahweh, was cap-
    tured in their pits,
    Of whom we said, 'In his shadow we shall live among the
    nations.'

21. *Šin*
    Rejoice and exult, O daughter of Edom, you who dwell in the
    land of Uz!
    For unto you the cup shall pass, you shall become drunk and
    lay yourself bare!

22. *Taw*
    Your guilt is at an end, O daughter of Zion, he will never again
    carry you into exile!
    He will punish your iniquity, O daughter of Edom, he will
    expose your sins!

CHAPTER FIVE

1. Remember, O Yahweh, what has happened to us! Behold and
   consider our reproach!
2. Our inheritance has been turned over to foreigners, our houses
   to strangers.
3. We have become orphans without fathers, our mothers have
   become as widows.
4. Our drinking water costs us, our firewood comes at a price.
5. Upon our very necks we are pursued, we grow weary and have
   no rest.
6. To Egypt we extended the hand, to Assyria for a sufficiency of
   bread.
7. Our fathers sinned and are not, we bear their guilt.
8. Servants rule over us, no one delivers us from their hand.
9. At the peril of our lives we get our food because of the sword
   in the wilderness.
10. Our skin is hot as an oven because of the ravages of hunger.
11. Women have been ravished in Zion, maidens in the cities of
    Judah.
12. Princes have been hung by their hands, elders are not honoured.

13. Young men have borne the hand-mill, and boys stumble under loads of wood.
14. Elders are gone from the gate, young men from their music.
15. The joy of our heart has ceased, our dancing has been turned to mourning.
16. The crown has fallen from our head; woe to us, for we have sinned!
17. Because of this our heart is faint, because of these things our eyes are darkened.
18. Upon Mount Zion, which is desolate, jackals stalk about.
19. Thou, O Yahweh, dost endure forever, thy throne to generation on generation!
20. Why dost thou continually forget us, forsake us unendingly?
21. Turn us, O Yahweh, unto thyself and we shall be turned! Renew our days as of old!
22. Or hast thou utterly rejected us? Art thou exceedingly angry with us?

INTRODUCTION

IN spite of the efforts of C. C. Torrey to prove otherwise,[1] the events of the sixth century B.C. had a profound effect upon Hebrew religion, so much so that we are justified in continuing the conventional division of pre-Christian time into pre-exilic and post-exilic ages. The destruction of Jerusalem, the loss of statehood, the deportation of the leaders, and the cessation of cultic religion were epochal events for they marked the end of one era and the beginning of another. From this congeries of events developed Judaism with its primary emphasis on law piety and with its various wisdom and apocalyptic movements. It is a glaring *non sequitur* that because the Chronicler exaggerated the importance of the exile and restoration he therefore invented them. Both Jeremiah and II Kings frankly admit the relative *numerical* insignificance of the deportations but both are clear in their testimony to the exile's historical and religious importance. The collective witness of Ezekiel, Second Isaiah, Haggai and Zechariah only furthers this impression.

As a matter of fact, by using Torrey's methods, it can be similarly demonstrated that, in virtue of the size of the armies involved, the American Revolution was of small consequence. Surely an interpretation that must depend so heavily upon quantitative measurement is a superficial one. If the enduring memory of events and their impact upon succeeding generations is the major criterion of historical importance, then there can be no doubt that the sequence of happenings from 597 to 538 B.C. were among the most fateful in all Hebrew-Jewish history. Is it far wide of the mark to recognize in the sixth century B.C. the severest test which Israel's religion ever faced?

The significance of the Book of Lamentations consists in its close connection with the tumultous events of that era and its vital interpretation of the flux of contemporary history. It is regrettable that Old Testament study has failed to see this im-

---

[1] Torrey's theory is most fully set forth in *Ezra Studies* (Chicago, 1910) but it receives further documentation in *The Second Isaiah. A New Interpretation* (Edinburgh, 1928).

portance. Most treatments of Lamentations have been content
to argue and reargue the Jeremianic authorship. It is as though
scholarship had been satisfied to debate whether or not Isaiah of
Jerusalem had written Isa. 40-66 without ever going on to probe
the religious import of those chapters. The study of Lamentations has been arrested at just such a critical level, and no really
constructive interpretative work has been undertaken. Back of the
present study lies the conviction that the document is a primary
source for an understanding of Hebrew religion. It has particular
relevance for one who would enquire into the survival value of
Old Testament faith. The need for this sort of study becomes all
the more urgent when we consider that nearly all the books
written on the history and religion of the exile totally bypass, or
at best, only casually mention the composition.

Does the present study claim to be an advance upon the several
reputable commentaries which are available?[1] The answer consists in the difference of approach and organization, and therefore,
in result. The primary obligation of a commentary is to elucidate
the meaning of the text by an exegesis of the successive verses.
Introductory to this task are the literary and historical questions
which serve to place the document in its proper milieu. In practice, however, it has often meant that the over-all significance of
the work is sacrificed to a piecemeal analysis. Pressed by lack of
space, the treatment of literary character, historical setting and
theological importance is frequently consigned to a few scant
pages. This is the peculiar fate of the shorter Biblical books.
Nowhere has this been more evident than in Lamentations, often
regarded as a relatively inconsequential supplement to Jeremiah.
The commentators have been more at pains to show us that
Jeremiah could not have written the book than they have been
interested in articulating the message, whoever the author (or
authors) may have been.

With this serious omission in mind, a new approach is in order.
Many of the shopworn topics of debate, ceaselessly handled by

---

[1] Among the better commentaries are Eduard Nägelsbach, *The Lamentations of
Jeremiah* (New York, 1871); C. F. Keil, *The Lamentations of Jeremiah* (Edinburgh,
1874); Samuel Oettli, *Die Klagelieder* (Nordlingen, 1889); Karl Budde, *Die fünf
Megillot* (Tübingen, 1898); A. S. Peake, *Jeremiah and Lamentations* (Edinburgh, 1912);
A. W. Streane, *Jeremiah and Lamentations* (Cambridge, 1913); Max Löhr, *Die Klage-
lieder* (Tübingen, 1923); Wilhelm Rudolph, *Die Klagelieder* (Leipzig, 1939); Max
Haller, *Die Klagelieder* (Tübingen, 1940).

the commentaries and introductions, will be scarcely touched upon in the following pages. In order to clear the way for fruitful study, the author wishes to make it plain that he does not believe that Jeremiah wrote Lamentations, nor is he satisfied with the usual critical alternative: three or more authors over a period of perhaps two centuries. He believes that at least the first four poems (which correspond to the first four chapters) are the work of a single poet. With respect to the concluding poem it is impossible to be dogmatic. All of the poems, however, are to be understood as stemming from the exilic period between 586 and 538 B.C. The uniform historical setting, the similarities of style and vocabulary, and the community of thought which they share make it possible to speak of *the theology* of the Book of Lamentations. This would be true even though on secondary historical and literary grounds we should conclude that there were as many as five poets responsible for the finished product. We would then be forced to recognize a school of thought.

The aim of this monograph is to show in some detail that the Book of Lamentations has significance as the literary deposit of a critical historical era, that it possessed an important communal function and proclaimed a vital faith capable of adaptation to the storm and stress which attended the passing of the Hebraic Age. The writer has found himself repeatedly driven beyond the external questions of integrity, date, style, literary type and cultic usage, to the deep emotions and sincere faith that motivated the book's composition. It is his contention that in the theological conceptions and religious motivations of the poet or poets the work achieves its clearest unity and its greatest value for Old Testament study. One need not force or fabricate such unity; it need only be discovered and interpreted. In particular, attention will be called to the acrostic form and the literary type, which in Lamentations are not only in themselves fascinating, but can be fully understood only as the vehicles of certain definite religious conceptions.

The writer hopes that some who have thought of Lamentations (if indeed they have thought of it at all!) as the dreary sobbing of Jeremiah over the ruined city or as a mere appendage to the prophet's book, will be led to a fuller appreciation of its literary qualities, its utter sincerity and its unyielding, courageous faith.

Introduction

To the student of Hebrew religion a right understanding of the Book of Lamentations will open new vistas on the crucial period of the exile when exuberant Hebraism issued in chastened Judaism.

THE ACROSTIC FORM

THE Book of Lamentations is a studied literary creation whose intricate construction has been carried out more thoroughly and elaborately than perhaps any other Old Testament book. Even an untrained eye can readily recognize the peculiar rhythm. The first four poems are composed of lines unequally divided, the first hemistich (or half-line) being the longer. All critics agree that these four chapters are of a like metre, although it has never been an easy task to define that rhythm with justice to its variations. Ever since Budde[1] the metre has been identified as basically a 3/2 stress. The so-called *Qinah* or lament metre is seldom found, however, in a rigid form, inasmuch as it is constantly being broken by a 2/2 or 2/3 or 3/3 pattern. The final poem is without doubt the more familiar 3/3 rhythm.

But of special concern is the acrostic form of the composition. Of the fourteen acrostics (or partial acrostics) found in the Old Testament,[2] the Book of Lamentations stands alongside of Psalm 119 as the largest in scope and execution. It is incomparably the finest in its careful detail and subtlety of development. Perhaps Psalm 119 is the more architecturally imposing with its twenty-two stanzas of eight lines each, every line beginning with the appropriate acrostic letter. Yet the very unrelieved severity of its form is oppressive and a single reading will disclose its didactic and gnomic character. Psalm 119 is properly an acrostic tour de force which does not approach literary or poetic excellence. Lamentations too has an architectural grandeur, but it is not monolithic. Like a great cathedral, its unity is broken in innumerable pleasing ways, never distracting but always contributing to the total impression. Actually the acrostic in Lamentations has 266 lines, exceeding the psalm by 90 lines, and yet with the former we are never conscious of length as we are so painfully aware in the latter.

[1] Karl Budde, 'Das hebräische Klagelied', *ZAW* 2 (1882), pp. 1-52.
[2] The canonical acrostics are Nahum 1.2-8; Psalm 9-10, 25, 34, 37, 111, 112, 119, 145; Prov. 31.10-31; and Lam. 1-4. Cf. Max Löhr, 'Alphabetische und Alphabetisierende Lieder im Alten Testament', *ZAW* 25 (1905), pp. 173-198; Franz Dornseiff, *Das Alphabet in Mystik und Magie* (Leipzig, 1922), p. 147.

We begin with the basic fact that each of the first four poems is a complete acrostic, i.e. one which employs all twenty-two letters of the Hebrew alphabet. It is also obvious that the fifth poem, while not an acrostic, has been accommodated to the acrostic scheme by having twenty-two lines, in exact correspondence to the number of letters in the alphabet. From this point of view it may properly be called alphabetic. Upon further examination, it is evident that chapters one, two and three are identical in that they are composed of three-line strophes. The fourth poem, with two-line stanzas throughout, is unique. Chapter three, the central poem, shares the feature of Psalm 119 previously noted: each line begins with the appropriate letter of the alphabet, with the result that there are three *aleph* lines, three *beth* lines, etc. In chapters two to four we find a curious and unexpected disturbance of alphabetic order: the acrostic stanzas appear in the order *pe-ayin*. If this peculiar sequence were characteristic of any one chapter we could explain it as a scribal error of transposition, but are we to believe that such an accident occurred three times? If anything, the normal *ayin-pe* arrangement in the first poem is to be attributed to a scribal slip.

The apparent contradiction between artificial literary form and spontaneity of emotion has attracted the attention of successive generations of commentators on Lamentations. Both factors are present to a remarkable degree, constituting an unparalleled situation, at least in the Old Testament.[1] On the one hand, the alphabet is repeated four times with unvarying regularity. On the other, the sincerity and directness of emotion cannot be denied. In the composition of Lamentations there has been a surprising coalescence of form and vitality. It is true that Ps. 9-10, 25, and 34 have some stirring sections, but they scarcely compare with the torrent of emotion that sweeps through Lamentations. The remaining Old Testament acrostics are more definitely in the quietistic vein of the Wisdom literature.

Inevitably the question occurs to us: what was in the mind of the poet that he should deliberately subject his expression to such

[1] E. H. Plumptre, *Lamentations*. An Old Testament Commentary for English Readers (London, 1884), pp. 182 f discusses several Classical, Medieval and Anglo-Saxon compositions that combine high emotional and literary qualities with varying degrees and kinds of artificial form. None, however, offers a convincing analogy to the Book of Lamentations.

a strict and disciplined form? It has been conjectured that the original writing was unfettered by the alphabetic structure and only at a later time was moulded to its finished state. But this does not remove our problem. The fact is that the document as we have it preserves an impressive example of spirit controlled by form. So far as we can discern, the two are inseparable. That this peculiarity of form has long been recognized as of central importance is seen in the manuscripts of all the standard codices where space has been left between the strophes beginning with the respective letters.[1] So the question cannot be disposed of: why should grief and consolation submit to the acrostic strictures?

A possible explanation is that the acrostic witnesses to the magical power of the letters. It is widely known, of course, that letters, syllables, words, and phrases have been regarded the world over as having inherent potency to ward off evil and to secure benefits.[2] Jeremias says of the letters among the Jews that they were thought of as holy, directly breathing the spirit of God.[3] He derives this from the Babylonian idea that the entire alphabet represents the cosmic circle and possesses, therefore, a supernatural power. By studying the magical ideas associated with language we may undoubtedly learn something about the origin of the alphabet and the acrostic, but any direct transfer to Lamentations is doubtful. That this kind of magical potency was attributed to letters in the sixth century B.C. by the community of devout Jews is really unthinkable. We have absolutely no evidence that any of the Jews in this period were infected with the magical passions which were later to absorb the interests of the Medieval Cabbala. In a sense, this view also belies the thought of the book which is not reiterative to the extent that the author expected to be heard solely because of 'his much speaking'. If anything, what was originally magical, has been softened into a conventional style. And if this is granted, we still must ask: what led our author to choose this particular conventionalism? Another twist to this theory, equally unconvincing, is what we may call the allegorizing

[1] C. D. Ginsburg, *Introduction to the Massoretico-Critical Edition of the Hebrew Bible* (London, 1897), p. 20. H. B. Swete, *Introduction to the Old Testament in Greek* (Cambridge, 1907), p. 360 points out that the LXX codices also indicate the strophes, either by transliteration of the Hebrew, e.g. ἄλεφ, βήθ, γίμελ, or by Greek numerals.

[2] Alfred Bertholet, *Die Macht der Schrift in Glauben und Aberglauben* (Berlin, 1949).

[3] Alfred Jeremias, *Das Alte Testament im Lichte des Alten Orients* (Leipzig, 4th ed., 1930), p. 665.

of the magic power. This was advanced by the sixth-century Catholic scholar Cassiodorus who said: 'Jeremiah bemoaned the captivity of Jerusalem in a quadruple alphabetical Lamentation, indicating to us, by the sacrament of letters, the mysteries of celestial things.'[1]

This brings us to the theory that the acrostics in Lamentations are a pedagogic device. There was unquestionably a close relationship between Wisdom literature and the ability to write. The scribes were the truly wise. Munch, therefore, believed that the acrostics were model compositions (*Musterstücke*) by which schoolboys were taught the alphabet and he has buttressed his thesis with illustrations from Egypt and later Judaism.[2] In particular, he regards Lamentations as an exercise for practising the style of the funeral lament.[3] Rudolph's comment on this explanation is of pertinence: 'That Lamentations was composed for instruction because the teacher wished to practice with his students the style of the funeral lament, makes of the intense earnestness of these songs, written with life-blood, merely an exercise in style.'[4] In short, such a view makes mockery of the emotional dynamic and deep gravity which suffuse the composition. It is conceivable that at some time in its early history the book was employed in didactic circles; it is, however, unimaginable that it was written for such purposes.

By far the most frequent interpretation is that the acrostic, at least in the present case, was a mnemonic aid.[5] This is often coupled with a cultic estimate of the book. There is much in this view which commends itself. It avoids the pitfalls of the previous positions by offering a practical purpose for the acrostics without depriving the entire work of its literary and religious stature.

It is, however, in connection with the acrostic as a means of

[1] Quoted in Eduard Nägelsbach, *The Lamentations of Jeremiah* (New York, 1871), p. 17.
[2] P. A. Munch, 'Die Alphabetische Akrostichie in der jüdischen Psalmendichtung', *ZDMG* 90 (1936), pp. 703-710.
[3] *Ibid.*, p. 710.
[4] Wilhelm Rudolph, *Die Klagelieder*. Kommentar zum Alten Testament (Leipzig, 1939), p. 3.
[5] Cf. Robert Lowth, *Lectures on the Sacred Poetry of the Hebrews* (Boston, 1829), pp. 39, 318; Ferdinand Montet, *Etude Littéraire et critique sur le livre des Lamentations* (Geneva, 1875), p. 42; Samuel Oettli, *Die Klagelieder*. Kurzgefasster Kommentar zu den Heilgen Schriften Alten und Neuen Testament (Nordlingen, 1889), p. 199; A. W. Streane, *Jeremiah and Lamentations*. The Cambridge Bible (Cambridge, 1913), p. 355.

facilitating memorization that any view of the literary unity of the Book of Lamentations receives a severe testing. While the present writer believes that one poet was responsible for at least the first four poems, he does not believe that the anonymous poet sat down with the purpose of writing a composition which would consist of four (or five) parts. It is much more likely that the five poems were written separately for successive annual days of mourning over the fall of Jerusalem and later compiled, probably by the poet himself, as a cultic collection. Only on this kind of theory can justice be done to the fundamental similarities and the lesser but pronounced differences among the poems.

The clue for this line of approach is provided by an examination of the hypothesis that the acrostics are an *aide-memoire*. For the sake of clarity, let us assume for the moment that the book is a conscious literary unit composed of five parts. The value of the acrostic for memory would then be practically nil. Were the alphabet given only once, its usefulness might be acknowledged. It would, at least, assist the person reciting the work to get started on the correct word in each strophe. But with each repetition of the alphabet (four times in all) its helpfulness in this regard becomes more unlikely. How, for example, would one remember that בכו, *bākhô*, began the *beth-strophe* in chapter one, whereas בלע, *billaʿ*, was the proper initial word in the corresponding strophe of chapter two? Any possibility that the successive *aleph*, *beth*, *gimel* words, etc., are themselves in alphabetical order according to their second letters is dispelled by a brief consideration of the acrostic words. In conclusion, granted the systematic character of the acrostic sequence, the selection of particular words within that framework seems to have been a matter of sheer arbitrariness. As such, it would have confused as much as it would have facilitated the memory.

Furthermore, there are certain acrostic words repeated (e.g. איכה, *êkhāh*, in three of the poems; ו, *waw*, in four) which are clearly unexplainable on the supposition that the book is a calculated unity. If it were, one would expect either that the same word would be found in the *aleph*-strophes, etc., throughout or that a different one would appear in each poem following some kind of logical order. Yet the indiscriminate mixture of the words betrays an inconsistency which is damaging, if not fatal, to the theory.

But, if we recognize that the poems were written independently of one another, then the difficulty vanishes. They were learned and recited separately; therefore, it was only when compiled that the question of alphabetic confusion would arise. By then the form of the poems was so fixed that changes would be difficult. Moreover the capacity of the Semites for memorization was so phenomenal that slavish adherence to memory helps was unnecessary.[1] The delimitation of the length of the poems and separate strophes, as well as the alphabetic order, would be ample assistance.

Memorization, then, may have been one factor in the acrostic construction of the separate poems in Lamentations. But it is not a sufficient motivation. There remains the one purpose of the acrostic, which has been suggested by a few critics, but developed by none. It alone can offer a fruitful avenue of approach. The function of the acrostic was to encourage completeness in the expression of grief, the confession of sin and the instilling of hope. De Wette was apparently the first to hint at this when, concerning the acrostic form he said: 'The elegiac humour of the sufferer has here expressed itself with a certain completeness.'[2] Keil declared that the alphabetical arrangement was chosen '. . . to give an air of continuity as well as of exhaustive completeness to the lamentation, which constantly assumes new figures and turns of thought'.[3] G. Smit remarks that all of the letters may have been used in order to include suffering in its full range.[4]

This point of view can be developed by reference to a feature of the acrostic which Munch makes clear. For the most part, the Hebrew acrostic appeals to the eye and not to the ear. Ps. 9.2 f, Ps. 119 and Lam. 3 may be exceptions to the rule. He insists it is improper to consider the acrostic as a type of alliteration.[5] By listening to Lamentations one, two and four, and possibly even three, one would hardly be aware of the form. To

[1] W. F. Albright, *From The Stone Age to Christianity* (Baltimore, 1946), pp. 31 f remarks: 'As has often been emphasized by scholars, writing was used in antiquity largely as an aid or guide to memory, not as a substitute for it.' He illustrates with examples from classical antiquity, Islam, China, Judaism and Hinduism.

[2] W. M. De Wette, *A Critical and Historical Introduction to the Canonical Scriptures of the Old Testament* (Boston, 1858), Vol. II, p. 532.

[3] C. F. Keil, *The Lamentations of Jeremiah* (Edinburgh, 1874), p. 337.

[4] G. Smit, *Klaagliederen.* Tekst en Uitleg. I. Het Oude Testament (Groningen, 1930), p. 117.

[5] Munch, *op. cit.*, pp. 704 f.

state it in a positive way: the form of the acrostic is basically *conceptual* and not *sensual*. This is a departure from most Babylonian acrostics which really amount to syllabic alliteration and occur in refrains which have at least a quasi-magic quality.[1] From this, of course, Munch infers that the acrostic function among the Hebrews was pedagogic, but it is better to interpret his evidence in another direction. Jeremias gives us our starting point: 'When a person says the alphabet, he has thereby embraced all possibilities of words'.[2] His allusion to the Babylonian habit of enumerating all possible syllabic combinations in order to banish a demon by finding his name, in no way compares with Lamentations. But what is of great importance is the concept of the emergence of all speech and writing out of various combinations of a relatively small number of letters. The possibility of magical ideas clustering around this concept is not only great but probably inevitable. Yet to even the most rational mind, the reality is apparent and the mystery of it is not wholly lost.

Those who entertain this idea of completeness, therefore, instinctively feel that in naming the whole alphabet one comes as close as man may to a total development of any theme or the complete expression of any emotion or belief. If the subject is to be exhausted, the alphabet alone can suffice to suggest and symbolize the totality striven after. We find this sentiment underlying the Jewish *widui* or lists of sins and sinners used for confessional purposes and garbed in alphabetic form.[3] It is likewise the foundational idea of many of the piyyutim used in synagogue liturgy from the Talmudic period on.[4] One of the most noted of these is the twenty-two strophe, 220-line poem created by Yose ben Yose in the seventh century A.D. Used on the Day

---

[1] *Ibid.*, pp. 705 f and cf. the syllabic acrostic, 'A Dialogue About Human Misery', in J. Pritchard, *Ancient Near Eastern Texts* (Princeton, 1950), pp. 438 ff. Hedwig Jahnow, *Das hebräische Leichenlied im Rahmen der Völkerdichtung. BZAW* 36 (1923), p. 169 has also stressed the formal principles of the acrostic in Lamentations; it does not require the laws of sound but can only be appreciated by the eye. He regards the book, therefore, as intended to be read, and for that reason, as literature in the strict sense of the term.   [2] *Loc. cit.*

[3] Cf. J. Rendel Harris, *The Teaching of the Twelve Apostles* (Cambridge, 1887), pp. 82 f; Kaufmann Kohler in *The Jewish Encyclopedia*, Vol. 4, p. 219; J. Muilenburg, *The Literary Relations of the Epistle of Barnabas and the Teaching of the Twelve Apostles* (Marburg, 1929), pp. 102, 105.

[4] Arjeh Dorfler in *The Universal Jewish Encyclopedia*, Vol. 8, pp. 548 f, states that piyyutim is 'from the Aramaic paytana, "the poet", a term for all kinds of poetry, then applied specifically to religious poetry intended for use in the synagogue.'

of Atonement, it recounts the history of sacrifice from the patriarchal period to the time of Moses and is climaxed by the story of the high priest's performance on the Day of Atonement, into which a formula of confession is inserted.[1] Certain Jewish sayings about the law contain the same conception of the alphabet as the embodiment of totality and plenitude and, thus, of perfection. In the Talmud we read, 'Rabbi Joseph recited, "Read not *at my sanctuary*, ממקדשי, *mmqdšî* (Ezek. 9.6) but *at my saints*, ממקודשי, *mmqôdšai*", this refers to the people who fulfilled the Torah from *Aleph* to *Taw*'.[2] In a Midrash we find, similarly, 'Adam transgressed the whole law from *Aleph* to *Taw*', and again, 'Abraham kept the whole law from *Aleph* to *Taw*'.[3]

It is the belief of the present writer that the author of the Book of Lamentations selected the external principle of the acrostic to correspond to the internal spirit and intention of the work. He wished to play upon the collective grief of the community in its every aspect, 'from *Aleph* to *Taw*', so that the people might experience an emotional catharsis. He wanted to bring about a complete cleansing of the conscience through a total confession of sin. Even then his purpose was not spent. He was also determined to inculcate an attitude of submission and a prospect of hope. By intimately binding together the themes of sin, suffering, submission and hope, he intended to implant the conviction of trust and confidence in the goodness and imminent intervention of Yahweh. That this is the case is evident in the third poem where the acrostic form is intensified at precisely the point where hope becomes the strongest.[4]

It is especially fortunate that the Book of Lamentations has been compounded of five parts. The poet wisely did not try to fuse or rewrite the constituents so as to produce a more unified work. While not his original intention, the results of compilation have greatly enhanced the total effect of the work. From both

[1] Ralph Marcus, 'Alphabetic Acrostics in the Hellenistic and Roman Periods', *JNES* 6 (1947), p. 113.

[2] Quoted in the Soncino edition of *The Babylonian Talmud* (London, 1935-1953), *Shabbath*, Vol. I, p. 254.

[3] From the *Yalkut Reubeni*, a collection of Cabbalistic and Midrashic comments in Hebrew and Aramaic made by R. Reuben ben Hoshki Cohen of Prague (d. 1673) and quoted in Harris, *op. cit.*, p. 93 n.

[4] The third poem not only introduces each line with the proper acrostic letter; but, in addition, the central strophes (those most articulate of hope) use the same acrostic word two or three times in each stanza (cf. vv. 19-21, 25-39).

the artistic and religious viewpoints, he has attained a thoroughness and emphasis that otherwise might well be lacking. For example, an aspect of grief is not systematically described when it first appears, but is allowed to return again and again in the various poems, thereby contributing immensely to the passion and rugged power of the document. Had any one facet of the sorrow been fully exploited in a given poem, it might easily have descended to tedium and monotony. This lack of neat organization, this tumult of thought, is one of the very strongest evidences that the book stands close to the events and emotions it purports to communicate. Even so there are scholars who complain about the monotony of Lamentations.[1] One wonders in what more skilful way the Hebrew poet could have treated so tragic and uninviting a subject as the extinction of the state, with all its attendant horrors and suffering. By a series of backward and forward movements he has truly suited the expression to the fluctuations of grief and guilt. The agitated train of thought flows from the agitated spirit of the sufferer. Indeed, by the very fact that the poems were compiled, we have evidence that the community felt that no one of them was adequate to express the meaning of all five. The motive behind the preservation of the five poems is similar to that which dictated the preservation of four gospels in the early church. A completeness is achieved by the five poems together which no one alone could begin to approach.

Furthermore it should not be overlooked that the very use of the acrostic has enforced the most judicious economy upon the poet. Once having chosen the two or three line strophe, the lengths of his poems were predetermined. This constraint is probably largely responsible for the obvious compactness and concentration of emotion. Criticisms to the contrary, the poet does not linger sentimentally over the scenes of horror he describes. He passes quickly from vista to vista and from thought to thought. The acrostic, combined with the clipped *Qinah* metre, has left the impression of deep feeling that is disciplined and restrained. As with some of the patriarchal stories (e.g. the

---

[1] H. Gunkel, 'Klagelieder Jeremiae', *Religion in Geschichte und Gegenwart*, 2nd ed., Vol. 3, col. 1059; T. K. Cheyne, *The Lamentations of Jeremiah*. The Pulpit Commentary (London, 1885), p. 1.

sacrifice of Isaac and Joseph and his brothers in Egypt) and the narratives of David's court history (e.g. the death of Bathsheba's child and the murder of Absalom), the descriptions are unusually moving. They allude to and suggest more than they actually say; there is an excess of meaning over statement. The acrostic may have hampered an unfettered emotionalism but it has greatly enhanced the expression of controlled feeling. This is perhaps another way of saying that reflection has already begun to bring calm into the midst of wild and irrational grief.

We may summarize this chapter by restating what we believe to be the twofold purpose of the acrostic as employed by the author of Lamentations. First and foremost, it offered a literary form corresponding to the completeness of grief, responsibility and hope which he wished to communicate. As such it was an extreme measure for a drastic situation. Second, it afforded an aid to the memory. It is strange that no one has commented on the novelty of the artistic idea, for it is clear that Lamentations is the first Biblical acrostic on so ambitious a scale, if not the very first.[1] It is likely that the poet had few if any Hebrew acrostic prototypes at hand. If, as moderns, we find it somewhat difficult to appreciate his purpose, we must at least admire the artistic skill and feeling for his subject which led the poet to adopt so radical a form to convey his message. We may also commend his instinct for preserving the separate poems without efforts to unify them by suppressing their individualities. If artistic achievement is to be judged by the correspondence between intention and execution, then the author of Lamentations, within the limits he set for himself, was an artist of the first rank.

---

[1] Dornseiff, *op. cit.*, p. 147; Löhr, *op. cit.*, p. viii. Nahum 1.1-10 is presumably earlier than Lamentations, although both Dornseiff and Löhr follow Gunkel in dating it late (cf. 'Nahum 1', *ZAW* 8 (1893), pp. 223-244). As the passage in Nahum stands, it is not only an incomplete acrostic but the alphabetic order is mutilated.

CHAPTER TWO

THE LITERARY TYPE

THE careful delineation and investigation of the types or *Gattungen* instituted by Hermann Gunkel[1] and carried on by W. Baumgartner,[2] E. Balla,[3] H. Jahnow[4] and H. Schmidt[5] is the necessary background for an understanding of the literary type in the Book of Lamentations. To be sure, the major area of their labours was in the Book of Psalms, yet by their own admission and by simple comparison it is easy to see that the same types are scattered throughout many parts of the Old Testament. These scholars, therefore, were correct in regarding Lamentations as of one piece with the Psalter in respect to types and stylistic features.

Three of these types, the communal lament or *Klagelied des Volkes*, the individual lament or *Klagelied des Einzelnen* and the funeral song or *Leichenlied*, are ordinarily associated with the Book of Lamentations. Yet from the standpoint of the formal criteria it is rather difficult to define the poems. Gunkel himself vacillated between criteria of form and of content. The hymn, for example, has certain clearly marked stylistic features; but, on the other hand, the royal psalm is discernible only by the presence of the king—a matter of content. Gunkel acknowledges this confusion when devoting a place to the mixed types or *Mischungen*.[6] The problem in Lamentations is sufficiently complex that at least the first four poems belong in this latter category.

When we pursue the other line of approach which Gunkel developed, and enquire into the *Sitz im Leben* of the respective types, we are able to explain why the mixture of *Gattungen* is so pronounced in our book. This is particularly clear with the communal lament which arises out of some disaster affecting the

---

[1] Gunkel, *Ausgewählte Psalmen* (Göttingen, 1917); *Die Psalmen*. Handkommentar zum Alten Testament (Göttingen, 4th ed., 1926); 'Psalmen' in *Religion in Geschichte und Gegenwart*, 2nd ed., Vol. 3, 1930; and completed by J. Begrich, *Einleitung in die Psalmen* (Göttingen, 1933).

[2] Baumgartner, *Die Klagegedichte des Jeremia*. BZAW 32 (1917).

[3] Balla, *Das Ich der Psalmen*. Forschungen zur Religion und Literatur des Alten und Neuen Testaments 16 (1912).

[4] Jahnow, *Das hebräische Leichenlied im Rahmen der Völkerdichtung*.

[5] Schmidt, *Das Gebet der Angeklagten im Alten Testament*. BZAW 39 (1928) and in a shorter version in *Old Testament Essays* (1923).

[6] Gunkel-Begrich, *op. cit.*, pp. 397-403.

C

whole people. It may be famine, plague, siege, military defeat or captivity, but it must always be sufficiently all-inclusive and menacing to constitute a threat to the body politic. It need not be laboured that the catastrophe of 586 B.C. was the disaster par excellence in the history of Judaism. It became so storied that all of Israel's later exiles were 'Babylonian' and apocalyptists of subsequent ages pictured the destruction of their own times under the guise of the events of the sixth century B.C. This is particularly noticeable in the canonical Book of Daniel written *c.* 165 B.C. and the pseudepigraphic Fourth Book of Ezra from *c.* A.D. 100. It makes little difference when we date the earliest communal lament (e.g. Ps. 80, in whole or part, may date from the eighth century B.C.). A knowledge of the history of the last days of the kingdom should prepare us for the sudden importance which the *Volksklagelied* assumed during this tragic period. It is altogether possible that it was not a very numerous or vital type prior to the exile.

But for Lamentations the national lament is the *primary* type and, in one respect, the only type, for all that the poet says is occasioned by the common misery. That he selects other types, first the funeral song and then the individual lament, is really incidental to the overarching situation and purpose: in the midst of great calamity he seeks to give expression to the communal grief and suffering, the communal sense of sin, and he hopes also to awaken communal hope and trust. To this purpose he bends every resource, including the use not only of *Qinah* rhythm and acrostic form, but also literary *Gattungen* adapted to his subject. It is not necessary or even realistic to imagine that the poet was aware of mixing types. At least his materials and methods were not at the centre of his consciousness. His fusion of the types was dictated by the feeling that their peculiar associations, in the one case the funeral and in the other case personal adversity such as illness or social ostracism, offered categories by which the communal distress could best be interpreted.

As to the formal distinctions among the types, Gunkel characterizes chapters one, two and four as *Leichenlieder*, though national rather than personal.[1] Hedwig Jahnow has made a detailed study of these chapters within the larger context of funeral

---

[1] *Ibid.*, p. 136; 'Psalmen' in RGG, Vol. 3, cols. 1058 f.

songs and mourning customs not only from the Old Testament
but Arabic and some European sources as well.[1] He concludes
that only a very few of the peculiar stylistic forms of the old
Leichenlied (e.g. the Lament of David over Saul and Jonathan in
II Sam. 1.17-27) are preserved without change in Lamentations.
Among these few are the initial word אֵיכָה, *êkhāh*, 'O how!'
(cf. Deut. 1.12; Isa. 1.21; 14.4, 12; Jer. 48.17 and Ezek. 26.17),
the summons to weep (2.18 f), and the statement in the form
of a narrative of the different ones who suffer (1.14*de*; 2.10).
Others are lacking. For example, there is no announcement of
death and no clarification of who is actually dead, i.e. is Zion a
'widow' because Yahweh, her political allies, or her population
is 'dead'? Furthermore, while many of the motifs of chapters one,
two, and four are exhibited in the *Leichenlied* (e.g. the contrast between 'then' and 'now', the lamenting mother, the malicious joy
of the onlookers and the cry for vengeance), there are others that
cannot be explained except by the influence of the popular lament
(e.g. the appeal to Yahweh). The most distinctive thing about
the funeral song in Lamentations is the fact that in the service of
religious faith, elements appear which are absolutely foreign to
the funeral song *per se*: the appeal to the name of Yahweh, the
confession of sin and the introduction of prophetic hope. This
leads Jahnow to observe:

> Therefore, only in altered form could the funeral song ex-
> perience that most significant transformation which we find in
> Lamentations: the transformation of an originally entirely
> profane type into a religious poem.[2]

But if the funeral song required substantial modification to suit
the poet's purpose, why did he choose it in the first place? The
answer is close at hand in the scenes of death amid which he
wrote. Grief for the fallen is the most powerful single emotion
in these chapters and the funeral song was the most natural
vehicle of expression. Yet he did not follow it slavishly. For his
innovations he already had some precedent in the prophetic
literature (Amos 5.2 f; Jer. 9.20 f). Jahnow shows that the prophetic application of the funeral song was a radical departure from

---

[1] Jahnow, *op. cit.*, pp. 168-190.
[2] *Ibid.*, p. 170; cf. also Gunkel-Begrich, *op. cit.*, pp. 136 ff.

its normal employment. It involved a sharp discontinuity between speaker and audience; it was sung in advance of death and applied metaphorically to the nation so that the corpse was the whole people personified. The funeral song in Lamentations is necessarily sung after the event, but it is national, and it is this which disturbs the uniformity of style—a fact which Jahnow fails to recognize. The poet cannot describe the nation apart from the concrete instances of suffering and death that he beholds on every hand. The root of the confusion of type and imagery is not, as Jahnow brands it, the lack of '. . . the powerful originality of a unitary artistic conception'.[1] It is, in truth, born of the poet's struggle to relate the individual sufferings of maidens, mothers, young men, children and leaders to the suffering of Mother Zion. Before his very eyes the mourning rites are observed for the dead inhabitants of the city (2.10). This suggests to him the figure of the city 'as a widow', which refers quite as much to her social dispossession as to her loss of nearest of kin. We are not to look for a literal 'husband'.

Still it must be conceded that Jahnow is right about the lack of consistency in the imagery and type. In either of two ways the poet might have avoided it: (1) The mother of Zion figure could have been followed faithfully with all the dead citizens regarded as her offspring, as in 2.21-22. (2) The actual scenes of the dead and the rites in their behalf could have been lamented and described, as in 2.10, 20. Yet either course would have deprived the poem of basic elements. The former would have been so figurative as to lack pictorial power and concreteness. The latter would not have given expression to the communal feeling and pathos associated with Jerusalem as a defenceless and dispossessed widow. Perhaps a more skilful poet could have combined the individual and collective aspects with greater finesse, but we must nevertheless acknowledge the sound instinct of the sorrowing author who would not sacrifice a realistic lament in order to achieve artistry.

Recognizing the mixture of *Gattungen* in Lamentations, Eissfeldt has made an analysis of the poems.[2] The chief value of the classification is that it shows us the complexities and pitfalls of

---

[1] *Ibid.*, p. 172.
[2] Otto Eissfeldt, *Einleitung in das Alte Testament* (Tübingen, 1934) pp. 545-548.

categorizing. Thus, in chapter one, he finds vv. 1-11 to be a funeral song over Jerusalem; vv. 9*c*, 11*c*, 12-16 an individual lament; v. 17 a funeral song over Jerusalem; and vv. 18-22 an individual lament. When the passages are read, one discovers that what Eissfeldt has done is to call attention to the transitions in speech between the poet and people. It is apparent that the vv. 9*c*, 11*c*, 12-16 are individual laments from the point of view of their formal criteria, i.e. they describe suffering in personal terms: sickness, pursuit, burden-bearing, etc. (1.12-14). But these same strophes have features which are obviously national, for the speaker bewails her young men and women (v. 15), her children (v. 16), her priests and elders (v. 19), and is called the virgin daughter of Judah (v. 15). In other words, it would be better to recognize that in chapters one and two there is a polarization between the individual sufferings of the people and the collective personified suffering of Jerusalem. Both the funeral song and individual lament as formal types are employed here and there, but always in the communal sense. Type and imagery are, therefore, subservient to situation and intention.

The third poem has been the centre of heated debate regarding its correct *Gattung*. Is it an individual or communal lament? Do we have a suffering person or the nation garbed in the veils of corporate personality?[1] Löhr, who took up the problem in considerable detail[2], referred to the fluctuating tide of critical opinion before him, first for the collective interpretation (R. Smend; E. Kautzsch; G. Beer) and then for the individual interpretation (B. Stade; K. Budde). Löhr places himself among the 'individualists', but much more significant than the conclusion is the careful analysis of the poem and the theory of authorship proposed. His study was a milestone for literary research in Lamentations. Löhr pointed out that two individual psalms are found in vv. 1-24 and vv. 52-66 respectively and are interrupted by a long passage in vv. 25-51 where the 'I' is only superficially related to what precedes and follows. The fact that the 'I' in

[1] For the fullest treatment cf. H. W. Robinson, 'The Hebrew Conception of Corporate Personality', *Werden und Wesen des Alten Testaments. BZAW* 49 (1936), pp. 47-62; also A. R. Johnson, *The One and the Many in the Israelite Conception of God* (Cardiff, 1942).
[2] M. Löhr, 'Threni III und die jeremianische Autorschaft des Buches der Klagelieder', *ZAW* 24 (1904), pp. 1-6.

vv. 48-51 is in contrast to the people, forbids a national lament. We are to see in this speaker the poet who pours out his tears in intercession for his suffering countrymen. It is here that Löhr claims to discover the clue to unlocking the poem's vagaries.

The speaker in vv. 48-51 is none other than Jeremiah (cf. Jer. 7.16; 11.14; 14.11, 17; 15.11), who has been chosen by the anonymous author to deliver a kind of penitential sermon. The opening and closing psalms were selected because they are thought to express the life fate of the great prophet of Anathoth. In reality, Löhr insisted, these two psalms stem from fundamentally different religious situations: the former (vv. 1-24) pictures a man visited by God with great misery who finally is redeemed by faith; the latter (vv. 55-66) presents one who, in hardship because of the oppression of his enemies, experiences the help of his God and is confident that his tormentors will receive well-deserved punishment. In addition, these psalms had an independent existence and were incorporated by the post-exilic author (probably fourth century) who transformed them into an acrostic and introduced the transitional passage. The entirety is addressed to a situation of communal distress but it is an individual lament because Jeremiah is presented as the counsellor of submission and hope.

There is much in this view that is significant. Löhr wisely makes the situation and intention of the poet primary and seeks to show how disparate literary elements were joined together. The imagery surrounding the 'I' in the three sections is somewhat diverse, and the unity of the poem is largely in the deep impression which the plaintive figure of Jeremiah has made upon the author who, in turn, presents him as the exemplar of submissive suffering. In short, Löhr has seriously tried to account for the unity of conception and the unevenness of style and *Gattungen*.

Nevertheless, he has been led astray in some respects and in others has not gone far enough in discerning the poetic purpose behind the poem. For this reason, his conclusions are both misleading and inadequate. He treats the variations between the two individual laments as proof of their independent status, thereby explaining their imperfect assimilation to the thought of the author. But he must assume that a tortuous job of revision was required in order to shape the original poems into the acrostic form. In the third chapter that would have involved a change in every line; it is not only an unlikely but an unnecessary hypothesis. The appeal to composite literary elements which the author has not wholly mastered is no more adequate a solution for our problem than it was for chapters one, two, and four. It is really no answer at all to invoke the ineptitude of the poet.

The alternative solution is once again to investigate the *Sitz im Leben* of the poet. Löhr has rightly evaluated the specific purpose of chapter three, i.e. to inculcate submission and to arouse hope in the face of adversity. The poet started with only this purpose; he had at his disposal no individual psalms which he incorporated, but only an intimate knowledge of the individual lament style. In the high point of his discussion, namely the third poem, he heaps up figures from this individual lament style in order to express the maximum of suffering. Yet he is not conscious of *Gattungen*. He does not think to himself: now I will apply individual lament terminology to the national lament. He has not thought of 'purity of type' and therefore has been guilty of no crime or inconsistency in his literary treatment. As a matter of fact he even shifts to a Song of Trust (Vertrauenspsalmen)[1] in vv. 20-33 and to an outright national lament in vv. 40-47. Owing to the great crisis, there is a shattering of the normal or 'typical' forms of speech and they are mixed in order to gain maximum effect.

Likewise Löhr has too exclusively stressed the individual nature of the poem. He was justified to the extent that the prophet Jeremiah probably here functions as the archetypal sufferer and the one Israelite most expressive of the divine judgment.[2] But as the mixture of the literary types has suggested, the author is quite beyond the distinction between the individual and the group and is simply giving the profoundest kind of expression to the long-recognized Hebrew category of corporate personality.[3]

[1] Gunkel-Begrich, *op. cit.*, pp. 254 ff.

[2] Perhaps the earliest exponent of this position was Saadia Gaon. In the nineteenth century L. Seinecke was of the same opinion. Recent adherents, who document the theory in more detail, are Otto Eissfeldt, *Der Gottesknecht bei Deuterojesaja* (Halle, 1933) and Sheldon Blank, 'Studies in Deutero-Isaiah', *HUCA* 15 (1940), pp. 1-46. They emphasize the prophetic nature of the servant and Jeremiah as the special model. For a summary of this position v. J. Philip Hyatt, 'The Sources of the Suffering Servant Idea', *JNES* 3 (1944) pp. 81 f.

[3] So far as the present writer is aware, the only one to advance this idea was H. Wheeler Robinson, *The Old Testament: its Making and Meaning* (London, 1937),

Jeremiah is the individual sufferer without equal, but by virtue of his representative position as the great prophet who pleaded with and preached to his people, he is also Israel.[1] For this reason, the poet finds no dissonance in passing from v. 27 with 'It is good for *a man* to bear a yoke in his youth' to v. 40 'Let *us* search and examine *our* ways and return to Yahweh' and again in v. 52 to '*My* enemies relentlessly hunt *me* as a bird without cause'. Similarly there is no offence in the opposition between the sufferer and 'all my people' in v. 14, for Israel too as a personified sufferer was surrounded with those who mocked and despised her (cf. 1.2*ef*, 8; 2.15, 16; 3.45, 46). The so-called discord created by the speaker in vv. 48-51 is also explainable by the vacillation and tension within the concept of corporate personality. The prophet as an individual comes to the fore and is described as weeping in not only the manner but in the same terminology with which Jeremiah is pictured as weeping for his impenitent people (cf. Jer. 7.16; 11.14; 14.11; 15.1). The abrupt entrance of 'the man' (הגבר, *haggebher*), in v. 1 has been regarded as an impossible representation of Judah, yet Hosea refers to God calling his 'son' from Egypt (11.1) and Isaiah depicts Judah as a sick and bruised body in much the same terms as Lam. 3.1-17 (1.5, 6), and finally, there is the Servant in Deutero-Isaiah, in which book we

p. 143: 'This "individual lament" is, however, based on the conception of corporate personality, which enables the poet to pass from his own personal sorrows to those of his particular group or of the whole nation; he feels himself the representative and summary of all in their sorrows.' It is apparent, nonetheless, that Robinson does not regard Jeremiah as the sufferer in chapter three.

[1] By this line of interpretation the objection of arbitrary exegesis, so well stated by G. B. Gray, *A Critical Introduction to the Old Testament* (London, 1913), p. 165, is overcome: 'The attempt to find allusions in Lamentations to personal experiences of the prophet recorded in Jeremiah rests on the highly questionable method of taking one or two statements as literal in a series of statements which must be mostly figurative. One might just as easily identify the author with Jonah over whose head the water flowed (Jon. 2.3-5, cf. Lam. 3.54) but who wasn't cast in a dungeon as with Jeremiah who was cast in a waterless pit (Jer. 38.6 ff, cf. Lam. 3.53) but over whose head no water flowed.' In the first place, it must be emphasized again that we are not concerned here with the question of authorship. But, beyond this, Gray forgets that Jeremiah was an historic figure who made a great impression on exilic Israel and Jonah was not. To be sure, we cannot rest our case on the literalness of a few images but rather must appeal to the large amount of Jeremianic diction (cf. M. Löhr, 'Der Sprachgebrauch des Buches der Klagelieder', *ZAW* 14 (1894), pp. 36 f) and the representative stature of the great prophet in the eyes of later generations. Cf. also J. Köberle, *Sünde und Gnade im religiösen Leben des Volkes Israel* (München, 1905), p. 262, who maintains that the third poem represents the appropriation of Jeremianic religious individualism by a later age. The poet desires, in his opinion, to speak *e persona Jeremiae*. It was the practice of synagogue and temple usage that led to its national application.

also find a city personified as a woman (Babylon in Chap. 47).

Finally that which is perhaps the most important single factor in assessing the *Gattung* in Lamentations the third chapter, is the simple fact that it has been placed in the midst of four poems that are patently national. Eissfeldt aptly insists that this is at least the oldest commentary on our song which we have and there is no reason to trust this witness any less than later explanations and modern feelings.[1] While Smend was undoubtedly over-zealous in seeing the personified nation in nearly all of the individual laments, his judgment on Lamentations three remains the most satisfying.[2]

Thus the outcome of our investigation suggests that the formal literary types are useful as descriptions of the approximate categories into which the Hebrew poetry divides but they are incapable of providing us with ironclad rules. Basic to the analysis of any particular *Gattung* must be the historical standpoint, the motivation and thought of the author. They were after all the decisive factors in the writer's mind. It is always the danger of literary criticism that it will be content with a survey or history of the formal literary types. Sheer arbitrariness with respect to the types is not to be expected, and the very mixture of *Gattungen* in Lamentations is ample evidence of the freedom which the poet felt to adopt and adapt any form that might further his avowed purpose. The foregoing discussion has attempted to show that the funeral song and the individual lament were germane to his subject and that he employed them in sharp juxtaposition not out of clumsiness but out of a felt need for comprehensive development of a great and tragic theme. This mixture of the *Gattungen* reaches its climax in the third poem, a poem of which C. J. Ball has said:

> There is something arresting in that bold 'I am the man' and the lyrical intensity, the religious depth and beauty of the whole, may well blind us to occasional ruggedness of metre or language, abrupt transitions from figure to figure and other alleged blemishes, some which may not have seemed such to the poet's contemporaries.[3]

[1] Eissfeldt, *op. cit.*, p. 547.
[2] Rudolph Smend, 'Ueber das Ich der Psalmen', *ZAW* 8 (1888), pp. 49-147.
[3] C. J. Ball, 'Lamentations', *Encyclopaedia Britannica*, 11th ed., Vol. 15, p. 127.

And as in thought, so in literary type, this chapter provides the closest Hebrew prototype for the Suffering Servant Song of Isa. 52.12-53.12. The fusing of types cannot be charged to pedantry but must be attributed to emotional, and even ecstatic, intensity.

We have now established that the Book of Lamentations is a communal lament of mixed types from the sixth century B.C. The significance of this fact for the task of writing a literary history of the poetic forms and types of Israel may be greater than at first meets the eye. It is certainly true that no literary historical theory, including Gunkel's,[1] has met with general acceptance among Old Testament scholars. With very few exceptions the Psalms are not susceptible to precise dating, even within centuries. Our knowledge of daily life and the cult of ancient Israel as it related to the poetic types is still very indefinite. Finally we are never quite sure of the degree to which the figures of the lament are to be taken literally. Yet in the case of Lamentations we have poetic literature with a fixed date in which the individual lament figures have been transmuted into collective usage. From this vantage point one may survey the poetic literature and raise the question: how do our poems compare with the communal laments of the Psalter? What is their relationship to individual laments in Job and the Psalms? Is any historical sequence traceable? Have we any clues for writing the internal history of the poetic *Gattungen*?

Immediately there appear many conjectures which are intriguing but, at the present stage of our knowledge, beyond the realm of demonstration. Is it possible, for example, that the many affinities between Job and Lamentations (e.g. vocabulary, style, and even thought) are due to the fact that Lamentations is deliberately raising the problem of Job by applying the individual lament to the national situation? Two facts caution us against a hasty conclusion. In the first place, the hypothesis of such an early date for the Book of Job is not widely received.[2] Of even greater moment is the high probability that in place of literary borrowing we have to do with a common fund of technical lament terminology which was used in the laments of the Psalter, the Book of

---

[1] Gunkel-Begrich, *op. cit.*, pp. 415-432.
[2] R. H. Pfeiffer, *Introduction to the Old Testament* (New York, 1941), p. 677, vigorously argues for an early sixth century date for Job. Of the same persuasion were the earlier critics A. Dillmann, *Hiob* (Leipzig, 1891) and T. K. Cheyne, *Job and Solomon* (New York, 1893), p. 74.

Job and Lamentations. Thus one's suspicion of a closer connection between Job and Lamentations fails of proof.[1]

Yet we are not left entirely to guesswork. There are a few signposts here and there which may suggest the way toward a proper interpretation. In the context of the popular lament there are places where the first person briefly appears (e.g. Ps. 44.6; 74.12; 83.13). Gunkel was probably correct in regarding this as the figure of the *Vorbeter* or prayer leader whose own personality for the moment dominated the lament.[2] It is very likely that we must look to this cultic recitation of the lament for the origin of the stylistic representation of the nation as a person and vice versa. The social and psychological matrix for such an interpretation has been present in Israel's nomadic past. It only awaited literary articulation. The close identification of the public Lament leader and the people is graphically shown in later Judaism (e.g. Neh. 1.5-11; Judith 9.2-14).

Rather unusual is the scant number of laments from the prophets and the psalms which embody individual and national features. In Micah 7.7-10 (possibly exilic or later) and Jer. 10.19-21; 31.18 f the community speaks as an individual. The more striking instances from the Psalter are 77, 94, 102 and 129. Psalm 129 is the most clear case. The remaining three are not so forthright, but the likelihood is strong that they are more coherent and purposeful than an accidental combination of individual and national laments would suggest. Here the nation is to be understood as the 'I' speaker. And it is of particular relevance that Psalm 102 parallels Lamentations in its basic organization. It begins with an 'I' passage (vv. 1-11), exhibits a middle 'we' section (vv. 12-22), and reverts to a closing 'I' pattern (vv. 23-28), which is precisely the ABA structure of the third poem of Lamentations.

Whereas with Job we are not able to salvage the theory of an early date with certainty, the situation is quite otherwise with Deutero- and Trito-Isaiah. The former is commonly dated *c.* 538 B.C. and the latter *c.* 538-500 B.C. with possible fifth- and even

---

[1] S. R. Driver, *Introduction to the Literature of the Old Testament 9th ed.* (Edinburgh, 1913), pp. 434 f. discusses, with proper caution and reserve, the problem of determining the literary relationships among Job, Amos, Isaiah, Jeremiah, Lamentations, Proverbs and the Psalms.

[2] Gunkel-Begrich, *op. cit.*, p.124.

fourth-century additions. In other words, Old Testament scholarship has the good fortune in the case of Lamentations and Isa. 40-66 to possess two documents that have been dated by means of criteria other than a subjective idea about who borrowed from whom. With fixed dating possible, the literary relations of the two works become of immense interest. As Löhr indicated, the affinities between Lamentations and Isa. 40-66 are numerous, and a close study reveals many more than he mentioned.[1] Some of these are shared by other early writings and cannot be of much help in determining influence between the two books. But others are unique or nearly so, thus demonstrating to the satisfaction of the present writer that both Deutero- and Trito-Isaiah knew the

---

[1] Löhr, 'Der Sprachgebrauch des Buches der Klagelieder', pp. 41-49. In the following list of parallels those noted by Löhr are marked with an asterisk and in each case the Isaiah reference is given first: עון‎--חטאת‎ in an oracular comfort announcement (40.2; 4.22); '*āwōn--ḥaṭṭāth*, 'iniquity--sin'.

משפטי‎, of Zion's 'right' (40.27; 49.4; 3.59), *mišpāṭ*;

לשון בצמא‎, with reference to being parched (41.17; 4.4), *lešôn baṣṣāmā*, 'tongue with thirst';

שפך‎ (42.25; 2.4; 4.11), *šāphakh*, God 'pours out' wrath or anger;

תנים‎--יענה‎ (43.20; 4.3), *tannîm--ya'ănāh*, 'jackals--ostriches';

* שוב אל-לב‎ (44.19; 46.8; 3.21), *šûbh el-lēbh*, 'to call to mind';

* דמה‎--שוה‎, in a question formula (46.5; 2.13), *dāmāh--šāwāh*, 'to liken ... compare';

בת‎, applied derisively to the enemy (47.1; 4.21-22), *bath*, 'daughter';

ערוה‎ (47.3; 1.8), '*erwāh*, 'the shame of exposure';

* ישב‎--דמם‎ (47.5; 2.10; 3.28), *yāšabh--dāmam*, 'to sit, to be silent', with reference to mourning;

* הכביד‎ (47.6; 3.7), *hikhbîdh*, 'to make heavy';

* לא זכר אחריתה‎, with reference to the sinful 'daughter' (47.7; 1.9), *lō zākhar aḥărîthāh*, 'she does not remember her end';

ישבה אלמנה‎ (47.8; 1.1), *yāšbhāh almānāh*, 'she dwells as a widow';

* נתן למכי[ם] לחי‎ (50.6; 3.30), *nāthan lemakkîm leḥî*, 'he gives his cheek to the smiters';

עזב‎--שכח‎, the Lord's rejection of Zion (49.14; 5.20), '*ăzabh--šākhaḥ*;

* שבר‎--מי אנחמך‎ (51.19, cf. 59.7; 2.13; cf. 3.47), *šebher--mî ănaḥămēkh*, 'destruction ... how can I comfort you?';

בראש כל-חוצות‎ (51.20; 2.19; 4.1), *berōš kol-ḥûçôth*, 'at the head of every street';

סרו סרו טמא אל-תגעו‎ (52.11; 4.15), *sûrû sûrû ṭāmē al-tiggā'û*, 'turn away, turn away, unclean, do not touch!';

נגזר‎, applied to the sufferer (53.8; 3.54), *nighzar*, 'to be cut off';

* סבל עונת‎ (53.7; 5.7), *sābhal 'ăwōnōt*, 'bear iniquities';

* בכסף‎--במחיר‎ (55.1; 5.4), *bekheseph--bimḥîr*, 'with money--at a price';

* נגאלו בדם‎ (59.3; 4.14), *n`ghō'ălû, baddām*, 'they are stained with blood';

* הפך‎ with respect to a possession (60.5; 5.2), *hāphakh*, 'to turn over';

Book of Lamentations. In addition, the involvement of all the chapters of Lamentations suggests that as early as 538 B.C. the five poems formed a single corpus. If the assumption that Deutero-Isaiah wrote in Babylon is correct, then Lamentations must have circulated in the exile as well as in Palestine proper. Finally, it is to be noted that the many affinities between the two books often strike deeper than mere verbal parallelism. They reveal stylistic features and forms of expression (e.g. oracular comfort announcements, Isa. 40.1-2; 54; 62.11; Lam. 4.21-22; rhetorical questions inviting comparison, Isa. 40.18, 25; 46.5; 51.19; Lam. 2.13; statements of omnipotence in question form, Isa. 43.13; Lam. 3.37-39; ironic mocking songs against the enemy 'daughter', Isa. 47; Lam. 4.21-22; complaints of Zion against the Lord, Isa. 49.14; Lam. 2.20; songs bewailing national suffering under the figure of a person enduring great pain and ostracism, Isa. 50.4-9; 52.13-53; Lam. 1.13-15; 3.1-18).

The evaluation and interpretation of this data is very difficult, but there are a few conclusions which may not be amiss. It is clear that the theological (i.e. the idea of the corporate personality) and the cultic (i.e. the *Vorbeter*) prerequisites for the mixing of the individual and communal *Gattungen* were present in pre-exilic Israel. The first steps taken in that direction may be seen in the *Vorbeter* psalms and the prophetic personifications of the people (cf. passages from Micah and Jeremiah and also Amos 5.2 f). Yet the Psalms in which the mixing of the types is most sustained all seem to belong to about the time of Lamentations, for Psalms 77, 102, and 129 (94 doubtful) apparently presuppose the cataclysm of 586 B.C. Thus it is at about the same period in history that the longer and more conspicuous *Mischungen* are to be found.

* דרך גת, as a figure of divine judgment (63.2; 1.15), *dārakh gath*, 'tread the wine press';

* כרב חסדו (63.7, 3.32), *kĕrōbh ḥăsādhāw*, 'according to the abundance of his covenant loyalties';

* קצף עד-מאד (64.8; 5.22), *qāçaph adh-mĕʾ ōdh*, 'be extremely angry';

* כל-מחמדי (64.10; 1.7, 10, 11; 2.4), *kol-maḥmaddê*, 'all the precious things';

* פרש יד, in the sense of imploring or beseeching (65.2; 1.10, 17), *pāraś yadh*, 'stretch forth the hand';

שוש - - שמח (66.10; 4.21), *śūś - - śāmaḥ*, 'rejoice - - be glad'.

Acquaintance with the wider affinities of thought may be gained by a close reading of the following Isaiah passages in which occur many motifs familiar to Lamentations: 47; 51.17-23; 54.1-8; 64.

We must recognize, then, a community of thought in which the most appropriate way to express communal disaster is to apply the various categories of individual lament: sickness, hunting, waters of the underworld, etc.[1] We may, therefore, frame the tentative theory that the catastrophic events of the fall of Judah led to a deliberate fusion of hitherto comparatively separate types. It is immediately apparent that this process came to a climax in Deutero-Isaiah, particularly in the mocking song over Babylon (Chap. 47) and the final Servant Song (Chap. 53). If this be true, then the importance of these antecedent Psalms and the Book of Lamentations for an understanding of the literary type and even the theology in Second Isaiah should be taken into consideration.[2]

[1] Suggestive discussions of the individual lament imagery are to be found in Baumgartner, *op. cit.*, pp. 8-16, and Christoph Barth, *Die Errettung vom Tode in den individuellen Klage- und Dankliedern des Alten Testamentes* (Zollikon, 1947), pp. 76-122.

[2] For a brief discussion of the various *Gattungen* in Second Isaiah and their close connection with the theology v. Eissfeldt, *Einleitung*, 380 f. The forthcoming Introduction and Exegesis of Second Isaiah in *The Interpreter's Bible*, Vol. V, written by James Muilenburg, promises to develop this aspect more thoroughly.

CHAPTER THREE

THE KEY TO THE THEOLOGY
OF LAMENTATIONS

THE current revival of Old Testament theology can be fruitful only insofar as it takes with complete seriousness the history of Israel's religion. If the past century and a half of critical study teaches us anything, it is that efforts to escape the historical milieu of the Old Testament or to renounce the historical method in Biblical study, lead not only to false literary-historical conclusions but also involve the very theology in inevitable perversion. The religious meaning of the Old Testament is not to be set over against the literary and historical meaning, as though they are opposite poles. While the theological treatment of the Old Testament calls for a larger measure of insight and empathy than strictly philological study, the fact is that the methods of responsible analysis and exegesis required for settling questions of authorship, date and provenance are not basically different from the methods of theological study. The latter must of necessity build upon the former. Finally, the religious meaning of the Old Testament must remain essentially opaque to one who has not familiarized himself with the ever-changing literature and history of Israel. Let it be noted that this warning is not merely the hue and cry of historians. It has been sounded by Biblical theologians who remind us that the theology of the Old Testament is not an ideational system of dogma, but is basically the interpretation of Israel's historical life. The self-understanding of the covenant people presupposes a knowledge of the history of Israel. Of no religion in all the world is it so nearly true that to know the history is to know the faith.

Among the epochal historical events and movements that shaped Israel's faith were the Egyptian sojourn and exodus, the invasion and gradual conquest of Palestine, the cultural encounter between Yahwism and Baalism, the establishment of the monarchy and its slow decay, the collapse of national independence and Israel's engulfment by the world empires. From within the Hebrew tradition, these occurrences and developments were read as a series of assertions and denials of the national faith in Yahweh.

47

The last, and most traumatic, was the slow attrition of the national state, beginning in the eighth century B.C. The decline of the Kingdoms of Israel and Judah represented a blatant denial of Yahwism and might have proven disastrous were it not for the prophetic movement which had foreseen and forewarned of the doom to come. In 586 B.C. the worst of the prophets' forebodings were fulfilled. The Book of Lamentations belongs to the final stage of this doom. It stands at the nadir of Israel's fortunes and, as might be expected, it is above all else a book about the tragedy which befell an historically-minded people.

The Book of Lamentations, then, like the Book of Job, is largely a book about suffering, but, unlike the latter, Lamentations is closely related to historical crisis. The theological significance of Lamentations consists in its bold and forthright statement of the problem of national disaster: what is the meaning of the terrible historical adversities that have overtaken us between 608 and 586 B.C.? How are we to read these events in the light of our past? What is our duty in this present? Are we to look for deliverance and a new life? Have the promises of Yahweh failed? Is he powerless or does he no longer care? What are we to make of God's nature and purpose? The answers of the believing community to these perplexities formed the warp and woof of exilic thought and eventually determined the fabric of Judaism. Had these urgent questions been solved otherwise than they were, Jewish faith would have had a very different orientation or might never have survived the hour of its greatest testing.

It is essential that we have the proper historico-theological perspective before concentrating on Lamentations. That which all students of the subject emphasize, in one form or another, is the centrality of suffering as the major problem of Hebraism and Judaism as well. By 'problem' we mean the issue that posed the greatest obstacle or threat to religious faith. This condition stems from the firm theistic temper of Old Testament religion, for, as its implied universalism developed, glaring violations of Yahweh's justice and love appeared on every hand. Direct divine control of the events of history was the passionate substance of that faith, but the serious challenge created by the chaos of unrequited evil and innocent suffering was more than even the Deuteronomic constructions could indefinitely gloss over. As long as a simple correspondence was assumed between virtue and reward, between evil and punishment—just so long suffering as a problem could not arise. Yet when the old coherences began to crumble, it was inescapable that the whole fabric of life's incongruities should be questioned. It is to the enduring credit of Israelite and Jewish religion that the case against faith was fully stated and thus, in the end, had its own contribution to make to faith. From the exile on, the Old Testament theology of suffering functioned as a sort of *via negativa*, leading always to the element of mystery in the workings of Yahweh.

As early as Israel's settlement in Palestine, forces were unleashed which would eventually raise the issue of irrational suffering, i.e. suffering that could not be accounted for by any accepted moral or religious theory. The passage from a nomadic social structure to a sedentary agricultural way of life was the initial step in the process of Hebrew social maturation and decay.[1] But there is no reason to believe that the tension between actuality and the theory of reward was sensed until sometime in the monarchic period. With David and Solomon, Israel was thrust upon the stage of world affairs not simply as a pawn but as a respectable participant. Hebrew economic life became increasingly commercial and property, both goods and land, was gradually concentrated in the hands of a powerful few.[2] Such gross dislocations of fortune raised far-reaching questions. It was observed that often the most thriving Israelites were the greedy and ruthless landowners and merchants, and, conversely, the dispossessed peasants were frequently the pious. As a matter of fact, in order to achieve worldly success, many Israelite land barons and commercial middlemen boldly defied the old nomadic mores which Yahwism sanctioned. The theory of individual retribution did not square with the evidence nor did the idea that the individual was bearing the punishment due to the nation seem applicable. Probably as these social and economic injustices were pondered, the inequities of natural evil began to clamour for attention. Previously, incongruous as sickness might be, it was always

---

[1] J. Pedersen, *Israel. Its Life and Culture* (London, 1946), Vol. I-II, pp. 12-29; R. B. Y. Scott, *The Relevance of the Prophets* (New York, 1944), Chap. VIII.

[2] E. Meyer, *Die kulturelle, literarische und religiöse Entwicklung des israelitischen Volkes in der ältern Königszeit* (Berlin, 1930), pp. 5 f; T. H. Robinson, 'Some Economic and Social Factors in the History of Israel', *ET* 45 (1933-1934), pp. 264-269, 294-300.

explainable by some secret sin unknown to the sufferer. But now it was asked: if the rich do not always deserve their wealth and the poor do not always merit their poverty, is disease necessarily a result of sin? Adding to the crisis in faith was the break-up of the old solidarity of the family or clan—a process hastened by the passage from nomadic life to the Canaanite monarchic system where each man was less a member of a family or tribe than he was a citizen of the state.[1]

The intolerable contradiction between the ancient faith of Israel and the discontinuities of history could not long go unresolved. What brought the issue to a head and made suffering the first concern of Israel was the succession of swiftly-moving events from 626 to 586 B.C.[2] Following the recession of Yahwism under Manasseh (693-639), Josiah promulgated the great Deuteronomic Reform based firmly on the proposition that righteousness exalts a nation. The Book of Deuteronomy may thus be understood as a deliberate restatement of the naive theory of retribution and reward long presupposed among the Hebrews. The genius of Deuteronomy consisted in its liberal appropriation of the prophetic teaching, on the one hand, and its expansive homiletical style, on the other, which rested the whole argument upon the authority of Moses and called for absolute loyalty to Yahweh, by virtue of which the covenant people would prosper and be blessed in the earth. Deuteronomy enunciated as the fundamental principle of Israel's religion God's control of history. It cannot be too strongly insisted that this principle endures as the bedrock of Jewish-Christian faith. But under the duress of polemical and apologetic needs, Deuteronomy goes on to state that history knows no exceptions to the will of Yahweh. Not only this, but the workings of Yahweh are transparent to any one who will observe. It is a striking anomaly that the Deuteronomist, who most explicitly invokes the mystery of Yahweh's love in the choice of Israel, is most thoroughgoing in his ruling out of all that is imponderable or mysterious in the working of Yahweh's will once he has entered into compact with Israel. It is no wonder, then, that orthodox rationalisms and moralisms, whether Jewish or Christian, continue to be nourished by the Deuteronomic

[1] Pedersen, *op. cit.*, p. 22.
[2] A. S. Peake, *The Problem of Suffering in the Old Testament* (London, 1904), Chap. I.

outlook. And so the lines were drawn, from which there could be no retreat: Yahweh and his faithful people Israel would be tangibly vindicated in history. Such a conviction, so neatly stated, is obviously open to empirical testing.

But how did history treat this deep conviction? Young Josiah, the finest king Judah ever had, was killed by Pharaoh Necho at Megiddo (608); his son Jehoahaz was deposed and the latter's servile elder brother Jehoiakim was set on the throne as an Egyptian puppet ruler. With the shift of the ancient Near Eastern balance of power to Babylon, Jehoiakim became the subject of Nebuchadnezzar, and, after an abortive rebellion in 597, his son Jehioachin, then reigning, and several thousand citizens suspected as politically dangerous, were deported to Mesopotamia. In 586, after another revolt, Jerusalem was besieged and starved into submission, King Zedekiah and the leaders were killed or exiled, and the defences and important buildings were burned or demolished. Judah was organized as a Babylonian province. Imagine the discrepancy between the historical optimism of the Deuteronomic Reform and the cynicism and despondency evoked by these reversals of national fortune! As one student has so well said:

> This series of disasters must have been too tremendous a strain upon the old theory of the interrelation between sin and suffering. Here was a pious ruler, bending his energies upon the observance of the law. The law book promises explicity that prosperity and long life are the reward of obedience. Why, then, does Josiah die in the prime of life? *Why does the nation suffer more than ever before immediately after its earnest attempt at reform?*[1]

It is precisely this tormenting question which the Book of Lamentations inherits, for it stands at the point in Israel's life where the tension between history and faith is, for the first time, most sharply posed. In coping with this tension Lamentations accepts the prophetic teaching, but with respect to the historical enigma of Israel's life, it foreshadows the Wisdom literature by pointing finally to the mystery of the divine ways. For this

---

[1] G. Kubota, 'The Problem of Suffering in the Old Testament', unpublished Master of Theology Thesis, Union Theological Seminary, New York, 1928, p. 16 (italics mine).

reason, Lamentations is a serious theological document. While it is a book about suffering, it is not, as popularly supposed, simply a reflex outpouring of grief, a protest against pain. Like Christ on the cross, the pain of the nails and the crown of thorns and the jeering spectators were not as great as the agony of the spiritual desolation. Lamentations reveals a deep sense of desertion by men and God and it confronts suffering as a threat to God's purposes in history and to the very life of faith. To complete our analogy, it is of course impossible to speak of a resurrection, but, like Christ, the nation is able to utter the cry of commitment, 'Into thy hands I commend my spirit.' It is both the spiritual decimation and the spiritual conquest of the third poem which make it such a towering achievement.

As might be suspected, our book is not an abstract disquisition on suffering, but has for its basic purpose the mastery of pain and doubt in the interests of faith. It is less a treatise in philosophy of religion than it is a pastoral tract. H. Wiesmann, the only scholar known to the present writer who has made a close scrutiny of the theology, emphasizes the fact that: 'The conduct of men in the face of suffering in our book is not uniform and fixed, but rather undergoes development and improvement. To effect this transformation is the chief task of the poem.'[1] The higher purposes which suffering serves may be seen in the various types of suffering which the book acknowledges. In place of any simple answer, Wiesmann sees several lines of interpretation: Expiatory Suffering (*Erziehungsleiden*), Conversion Suffering (*Bekehrungsleiden*), Purifying Suffering (*Läuterungsleiden*), Humbling Suffering (*Demütigungsleiden*), and Serviceable Suffering (*Dienstleiden*). But the weakness of Wiesmann's analysis is, that by considering suffering alone, without relation to the total message of the book and often in abstraction from the history of the period, his treatment becomes highly speculative at points and seems frequently to be prematurely interested in relating the book's message to Roman Catholic theology. This is by no means an unworthy enterprise but it ought not to be confused with a faithful interpretation of primary sources.

Now that we have found the situational key to the theology of

[1] H. Wiesmann, 'Das Leid im Buche der Klagelieder', *Zeitschrift für Aszese und Mystik* 4 (1929), p. 109.

Lamentations in the tension between Deuteronomic faith and historical adversity, we may consider the composition itself. By far the most striking structural element in the Book of Lamentations is the recurring theme of reversal. From the literary viewpoint, it is *dramatic contrast*, and from the theological, it is *tragic reversal*. The continual clash of feeling arising out of this contrast gives the work its overwhelming emotional effectiveness. Yet this device is not created *ex nihilo* by the poet. He has drawn upon clearly recognizable antecedents, although in his composition the scheme of tragic reversal has assumed the utmost importance and has in fact become the pivot around which the whole theological discussion revolves. To trace the origins of this reversal schema is in the nature of a prolegomenon to the theology, but an indispensable one.

We must begin with the earlier occurrences of the theme. Its roots are to be found in the *Leichenlied* or funeral song by which the Hebrews (as well as all Semitic peoples) honoured and mourned their dead. Jahnow observes that in the funeral song there are two basic themes. One is praise and the other is lament. Encomiums of the dead consistently emphasize certain features of the *past* glory of the deceased: his bodily excellence (Lam. 4.7, cf. Isa. 52.14; 53.2), his splendorous garments, the number of his wives and children, his riches and luxuries (Lam. 4.5; Ezek. 27.3 ff), his origin (Ezek. 19.2, 10), his esteemed position, his weapons (II Sam. 1.21 f; Ezek. 32.27), and the irreparability and incomparability of the dead (II Sam. 1.19; Ezek. 27.32; Isa. 14.10). Laments, on the other hand, bewail the sad state of the *present*: the unalterability and inevitability of the fate of death (Jer. 9.21; Amos 5.2; Ezek. 19.9, 14), the transitoriness of the dead (II Sam. 1.19), the incomprehensibility of death (II Sam. 3.33 f), the abandonment and defencelessness of the survivors (Lam. 1.1), the manner of death, especially if unnatural (Jer. 38.22; II Sam. 3.33 f; Lam. 1.19 f; 2.11, 21; 4.5), the infamy of such a death (II Sam. 3.33 f), and the malicious joy of the enemy (II Sam. 1.20). Far from being unrelated elements, the motifs of praise and lament were frequently placed in a definite scheme which Jahnow called 'das Schema "Einst und Jetzt"', i.e. *the then* and *the now*. By this means the starkest instances of past glory are deliberately contrasted with the most glaring examples of present misery and degradation. The effectiveness of both is doubled by their very incongruity.[1]

The purest and longest example of the true funeral song which the Old Testament has preserved is David's Lament over Saul and Jonathan (II Sam. 1.17-27). It is worth noting the way in which the theme of tragic reversal is treated. The motif is splendidly enunciated in the refrain which begins and closes the lament, 'How are the mighty fallen!' (vv. 19, 25, 27), and is developed in a series of briefly sketched images and emotions. David pictures the courageous abandon with which the ill-fated warriors rushed into battle even in the hour of their doom (v. 22). He speaks of their prowess and strength like that of eagles or lions (v. 23). He mentions their unbroken fidelity to one another (v. 23). The prosperity of Saul's rule is boasted of in the description of the luxury with which he clothed the court women (v. 24). They are the glory of Israel (v. 19). Finally he remembers the loveliness and charm that made them so popular (v. 23) and endeared them in a special way to David's heart (v. 26).

The tragic reversal is in the form of a commentary on the last word in the refrain, 'How are the mighty *fallen*.' The fall is the death of Saul and Jonathan on the heights of Gilboa (vv. 19, 21, 25). Although his sword was swift and terrible, the shield of Saul was 'not anointed with oil', i.e. not made sacrosanct against the enemy's blows and was thereby 'defiled' or smashed (v. 21). The trusty weapons of war have perished (v. 27). The beautifully robed and jewelled daughters of Israel weep sadly (v. 24). The Philistine enemy rejoices (v. 20) and even nature is invited to join in the lament by withholding the rain of heaven and the waters of the deep (v. 21). It is evident from this analysis that in large measure the peculiar effect of the song is derived from its sharp juxtaposition of and constant movement between the past and the present, 'the then' and 'the now'.

The motif as it appears in Lamentations is very complex. There is, to be sure, the primary and fundamental contrast between the former glory of Zion and her present ignominy. In this respect the book is in the direct line of descent from the old funeral lament such as we have just analysed. But there are two variations

[1] This paragraph is largely a summary of Jahnow, *Das hebräische Leichenlied*, pp. 97 ff.

of the theme, only one of which, in a rudimentary form, is found in the *Leichenlied*. The first of these mutations is the contrast between the present downtrodden state of Israel and the present exaltation of the foe (cf. II Sam. 1.20). The second, which completely transcends the narrow limitations of the funeral song, is the contrast between the expected future of Israel and the expected future of the enemy. This theme is actually the tragic reversal in reverse! The present roles of victor and vanquished are to be exchanged. It is the denouement of the tragedy of Israel's historical life. Each of these types of contrast merits closer consideration.

The comparison between past and present is developed in the best tradition of the funeral song, with one crucial difference. It is necessary to examine this difference and its implications in some detail, for it reveals at once the wide gulf separating our book from the profane funeral song, in spite of the admitted affinities. This is seen most readily in the fact that while death is present on every hand, the central subject of the lament, namely, Judah or Zion, is not dead. In other words, there is no corpse personified as in Amos 5.2. Jahnow observed this peculiarity when she noted that the widow Zion has no husband.[1] Yahweh is not dead nor is the nation itself deceased, a fact proven by the many fervent prayers. Thus the striking transformation in the case of Lamentations is that, as applied to the nation, the contrast is not between life in the past and death in the present but a contrast between glory and favour in the past and humiliation and destruction in the present, although it is important to recognize that one of the most terrible evidences of the present woe is the slaughter and starvation of Jerusalem's citizenry. The change is typified in the representation of the city not as a corpse but as a humiliated and mourning widow (Chaps. 1, 2) and as a persecuted prophet (Chap. 3).

These inconsistencies of imagery are assumed by Jahnow and others to show the artistic decadence of the poet. In so doing one must disregard the tremendous problem of transforming a profane *Gattung* into a vehicle of religious faith and doing it so skilfully that it retains artistic coherence. The theological conceptions of the poet were primary and he assimilated to his purpose those features of the funeral song which would further that

[1] *Ibid.*, p. 172.

purpose. He could not, however, regardless of the strict require-
ments of the literary genre, represent either the deity[1] or the
nation as dead, for the simple reason that the whole burden of his
message was the indestructibility of Jahweh's purposes of love
and justice and, in consequence, the seed of hope in a restored
Israel (3.20-36; 4.21-22; 5.19-21). Strangely enough it is the very
weakness and inconsistency in form that discloses the religious
superiority of the poems.

The opening verse of the book introduces us abruptly to the
tragic reversal of Zion. Formerly she was a populous and
honoured city, comparable to a princess. Now she is depopu-
lated, humiliated and subjected to vassalage, to be likened to a
lonely widow. The image gains particular force when we remember the poverty and social stigma of widowhood in the
ancient Near East (Isa. 1.23; 10.2; Ezek. 22.7; Lev. 21.14; I Kings
17.10-12; Job 24.3, 21). The image is carried through v. 2 where we
find her weeping without any comfort from those who previously
were her 'lovers' and 'friends', but have now become her foes.

With the statement, 'All her glory has vanished from the
daughter of Zion' (v. 6), we may compare the initial line of
David's Lament over Saul and Jonathan, 'Thy glory, O Israel, is
slain upon thy high places!' In each instance there is the sense
of irrevocable doom and finality. In each the 'glory' is Israel's
fallen leadership, in the one case, Saul and Jonathan, and in the
other, the princes of Judah.

To add to her woes Jerusalem cannot escape memories of her
past—a past which is vividly present in the very midst of adversity. In her sorrowing vision, the past and present are painfully
at odds with one another:

> Jerusalem remembers in the days of her affliction and wandering
> All her pleasant things that she had from days of old. (1.7)

And what is the content of this memory of 'the precious things'?

---

[1] Erich Klamroth, *Die jüdischen Exulanten in Babylonien.* Beiträge zur Wissenschaft
vom Alten Testament 10 (1912), p. 61, declares that the carrying away of the temple
vessels destroyed Yahweh's sovereignty, thus the city is represented as a sorrowing
widow. A little reflection, however, shows this view to be completely untenable.
Of course the destruction of the cult is lamented but Yahweh is already detached
from the cult, for how else could he be pictured as destroying his own temple?
Nothing could be clearer than the assumption of Yahweh's continued sovereignty
and what is presupposed in all the poems is categorically stated in 5.19.

It would appear exegetically sound to infer from the later statement:

> The enemy stretched forth his hand upon all her precious
>   things;
> For she has seen nations enter her sanctuary,
> Those whom thou didst forbid to enter thy assembly! (1.10)

that her most valued possession was her religious heritage of festivals, sacrifices and, above all, the Temple. Her greatest affliction, the supreme regret of her homeless wandering, was the destruction of the religious system with all that it entailed symbolized in the imposing Solomonic Temple.

The second poem opens with a statement of the theme of tragic reversal in the form of an image not unlike that of the Day Star in Isaiah 14.12. Yahweh has beclouded or eclipsed the daughter of Zion and has cast her splendour from heaven to earth. The figure is best understood if we think of Zion as a star which has been deposed from its place of honour on the heavenly vault.

> O how the Lord has eclipsed in his anger the daughter of Zion!
> Has cast from heaven to earth the glory of Israel!
> And has taken no thought of his footstool in the day of his
>   anger! (2.1)

Then there follow three lines that continue in the vein of this reversal; that is, they have in common the casting down or removal of what was upreared and exalted. The fortifications of the city have been demolished (2.2*cd*), the honoured king and princes have been unceremoniously cast to the ground (2.2*ef*) and the horn of Israel's strength has been cut off (2.3*ab*).

In the ensuing verses the theme of reversal is implicit in the description of the demolition of the city, but it becomes most articulate in the jibe which travellers level at the exposed and ruined city: 'Is this the city of which they said, "Perfect in beauty", "The joy of the whole earth"?' (2.15*ef*). That the phrases 'perfect in beauty' and 'joy of the whole earth' were proverbial for choice cities is suggested by their similar use for Jerusalem in Ps. 48.1; 50.2 and Ezek. 16.14 (cf. also its application to Tyre in Ezek. 27.3, 4, 11, 24; 28.12). No more effective means could be employed to express the radical contrast between 'then' and 'now' than this cry of the passers-by who cannot believe that the ravaged city is really Jerusalem. 'Is *this* the city?!' The undertones of jeering irony are unmistakable but it is still basically an utterance of sheer incredulity. It is more an exclamation than a question.

The most grotesque and even sadistic treatment of the motif of tragic reversal is that which pictures Yahweh as performing unnatural acts and profaning what is sacred. The supreme hurt is that the judgment of God is administered under the guise of favour. In 2.20-22 there is a fierce indictment of God, spared from blasphemy only by the brutality of the circumstances it describes and by the relentless and callous God which the whole poem has portrayed. The first strophe of the indictment protests the inhuman contrast between motherhood and cannibalism, between the right of sanctuary and the slaughter of religious leaders on holy grounds:

> Behold! O Yahweh, and consider to whom thou hast done thus!
> Shall women eat the fruit of their womb, their fondled children?
> Shall priest and prophet be slain in the sanctuary of the Lord?
> (2.20)

The final strophe tells of the vicious slaughter of the city's population, multiplied as it was to overflowing by country folk who sought refuge within its defences. The poet's superb but brutal irony pictures it as a religious convocation called by Yahweh. The people came hopefully, in jubilant mood. They expected help from Egypt, festivity and victory over the foe. But instead of a feast day it was a judgment day and none survived the orgy.

> Thou hast called as a day of festival sojourners from round about,
> And in the day of Yahweh's anger there is neither refugee nor survivor;
> Those whom I fondled and reared my enemy consumed. (2.22)

The element of reversal is not at once apparent in the third poem, for one must read through several strophes before it asserts itself. The misery of the moment is present in the most heightened form, but the past glory is held back by 'delayed action' until it suddenly appears in shocking opposition to the uniform blackness of the contemporary scene. The sufferings of 'the man' are first described in a series of images intended to convey the impression of maximum suffering, unparalleled pain, utter loneliness and rejection (cf. Ps. 22.1-18; Isa. 53.1-10). One almost forgets, under the intolerable weight of the misfortunes proclaimed, that this man is not a professional sufferer. He is no ascetic reveling in his self-inflicted deprivations nor a chronic cynic exaggerating his troubles. Least of all can he be explained as a person undergoing ritual humiliation as did the Babylonian king in the New Year's Festival.[1] He is a man who once knew 'peace' (שלם, *šālôm*), 'hope' (לתוחת, *thôḥelĕth*), and 'glory' (נצח, *nēçaḥ*), but he has been 'rejected' from peace and his glory and hope perish. He has been wilfully tormented and afflicted by God and systematically reduced to a state of near despair.

As with the earlier poems, so with the fourth, we meet the dramatic contrast between past and present. One by one the various groups pass in review. We are first introduced to the precious sons of Zion who like gold are now tarnished and poured out in the streets (4.1). Once valued as priceless metals, they are now dishonoured as potsherds—by all odds the commonest and cheapest refuse of ancient city life (4.2). The upper class, royally apparelled and feasted on delicacies, are now scattered in the streets, dead of starvation (4.5). Princes whose beauty and health of body were the pride of the city are now blackened and shrivelled from the famine's terrible effects (4.7-8). The 'hands' of compassionate women (as though against their will!) boil their children for food (4.10). Priests and prophets who shed the blood of the righteous are themselves defiled with blood (4.13-14). Those who once doted on their every word as a 'vision from Yahweh' now banish them from the city with the leper's cry, 'Unclean! Unclean!' (4.15). The king, God's unique representative and protector of his people, like a weak animal of the wild, is captured in the pits of the wily foe (4.20). Even the 'overthrow' of Sodom and Gomorrah is no comparison for the tragic reversal of Zion (4.6).

In the closing poem, the incongruity of past and present under-

---

[1] Cf. the programme of the Babylonian New Year celebration in Pritchard, *Ancient Near Eastern Texts*, pp. 331-334.

lies the whole composition but is notable in v. 2, where the Jewish property owners witness the expropriation of their homes and lands, and in vv. 14-16, where the rule of the elders and the gaiety of music have departed from the city gates. Furthermore, the motif of tragic reversal is presupposed in the closing verses, where there is a fervent prayer that the tragic present may give way to a glorious future not unlike the remembered past.

In our consideration of the remaining two aspects of tragic reversal we shall first call attention to the intensity of the sting of defeat reflected in the contrast between Jerusalem's downfall and the enemy's exaltation. The broad implications of this reversal shall be more fully expounded in the next chapter. For the moment it is sufficient to observe that, not only was the memory of her former glory a source of constant vexation to Jerusalem, but the presence of the gloating and victorious foe was doubly galling. It is especially irritating when represented as a part of the divine plan. So the triumph of the enemy is mentioned as one of the ways in which Yahweh punished Zion for her transgressions (1.5). But the final insult is that the descent of Zion is accomplished by the ascent of the enemy (1.9), and the mockery and growing might of the hated Chaldean is attributed to the direct action of God: 'and he caused the enemy to rejoice over you: he has exalted the strength of your enemies' (2.17*ef*).

The final form of the tragic reversal is one earlier characterized as 'tragic reversal in reverse', i.e. the direct opposite of the present state of affairs shall prevail in that future time in accordance with God's will. The foes of Israel shall be punished as Israel is now punished and Israel shall rejoice as the enemy now rejoices. This is of course intimately connected with the ideas of vengeance and Day of Yahweh, but it raises its own questions. The finale of the first chapter is a passionate prayer for Yahweh's day of judgment to be unleashed against the enemy who deserves a fate the equal of Zion's in consideration of his iniquities. There is a definite bitterness in this cry, the bitterness born of Zion's pain and aggravated by the callous taunts of the victor. But there is also a strain of ethical and religious conviction, as we shall shortly emphasize.

The imagery of the individual lament in the third poem closes in a prophetic frenzy with the poet envisioning the complete requital of the suffering nation. It is so firm a conviction of the writer that he uses the perfect tense to describe the salvation of Yahweh which has snatched him from the derisive jests, the bitter vengefulness and physical violence of the foe. The final strophe is a curse directed against the enemy and is relieved only by the plea that their reward be 'according to the work of their hands', but it is obvious that the reward expected is complete annihilation and oblivion. The curse that rested for so long on the suffering 'man' (3.1-18, 52-54) is soon to be laid upon his enemies.

In chapter four we find the cup of Yahweh's wrath. The daughter of Zion has had her fill and henceforth it shall pass to the daughter of Edom. In a prankish play on words the poet announces that Israel 'will no more go into exile' (לְהַגְלוֹתֵךְ, *lehaghlôthēkh*) but Edom's sins 'will be uncovered' (גִלָּה, *gillāh*). The cup of the divine fury is a familiar prophetic figure (Hab. 2.16; Ezek. 23.31-33; Isa. 51.17, 22-23) and in two passages it is associated with an appalling judgment on Edom:

> For thus says the Lord: 'If those who did not deserve to drink the cup must drink it, will you go unpunished? You shall not go unpunished, but you must drink. For I have sworn by myself, says the Lord, that Bozrah shall become a horror, a taunt, a waste, and a curse; and all her cities shall be perpetual wastes . . . Edom shall become a horror; every one who passes by it will be horrified and will hiss because of all its disasters' (Jer. 49.12-13, 17).

For as you have drunk upon my holy mountain,
    all the nations round about shall drink;
they shall drink, and stagger,
    and shall be as though they had not been (Obad. 16).

Edom in these passages may be simply an archetype of Israel's enemies as it certainly eventually became[1]; however, it would be perfectly apt as a reference to the Edomite nation whose people pushed into the Negeb and the Hebron highlands during the exile.[2]

In conclusion, it is not overestimating the centrality of the

---

[1] Joseph Lury, *Geschichte der Edomiter im biblischen Zeitalter* (Berlin, n.d.), p. 67.
[2] W. O. E. Oesterley and T. H. Robinson, *History of Israel* (Oxford, 1932), Vol. 2, p. 55.

category of tragic reversal to assert that nearly all of the other motifs are not only related to it in one way or another, but that they actually find their mode of expression within its framework. The theology of doom and hope which suffuses the Book of Lamentations must be seen structurally in terms of the schema of tragic reversal. We have already had occasion to mention its close connection with the themes of reproach, vengeance, and Day of Yahweh. Others may be singled out. The steadfast insistence on God's righteousness and goodness declares itself in the conviction that as there has been a past glory and a present pain there will be a future return marked by God's favour (3.31-36; 4.22; 5.21). Likewise the moment of the restoration of Israel's historical life begins when she has made full satisfaction for her guilt (4.11*ab*, 22*ab*). Then and only then will the tide of fortune turn in her direction. Within this one motif there is an effective witness to the Hebrew's serious respect for all historical happening. There is a past, a present, and a future. The present has been unusually severe and bitter and thus the ground for grief and lamentation (1.8, 12, 17-18; 2.13, 18-22; 3.19, 43-51; 5.1, 20). But the future holds promise of restoration and therefore the basis for hope (3.20-36; 4.22; 5.21). Yahweh's lordship over history and his purposes are faithfully adhered to (3.31-36; 5.19). By these considerations the Book of Lamentations is imbued with greater significance than would be a mere lament. It rises far above pathos, for it insists on the coherence of history in the will of God who has the good of his creation ever in view.

CHAPTER FOUR

THE THEOLOGY OF DOOM

THE fall of Jerusalem was a clarion call to the entire re-thinking of Hebrew religion. In the truest sense this historic crisis was unparalleled in all Israel's history. At no time in the four-hundred years of the monarchy, with the exception of the brief raid of Shishak (c. 935), had the sacred city of Jerusalem been captured, much less destroyed, nor had the theocracy been interrupted. Now the sombre announcements of the prophets had come to pass. To the exile of king and leaders and the destruction of the city were added famine and slaughter. To an historical faith this catastrophe could well have been fatal. A survey of exilic literature, wherein is embodied the responses of Israel to the crucible of national calamity, makes it abundantly clear that Lamentations is far from being a case of literary exaggeration or warped hypochondria.[1]

One of the first to observe the grand scale of the tragedy lamented in our book was Bishop Lowth who said:

> Grief is generally abject and humble, less apt to assimilate with the sublime; but when it becomes excessive, and predominates in the mind, it rises to a bolder tone, and becomes heated to fury and madness. We have a fine example of this from the hand of Jeremiah when he exaggerates the miseries of Zion.[2]

Wiesmann, noting the same fact, remarked: 'The sensual nature comes into its own, indeed appears in its complete weakness: the travails of suffering find full expression, according to Oriental manner, with a certain extravagance.'[3] This 'fury and madness',

---

[1] Cf. esp. James Muilenburg, 'The History of the Religion of Israel', *The Interpreter's Bible*, Vol. I, p. 331. J. C. Todd begins his *Politics and Religion in Ancient Israel* (London, 1904) with this sweeping claim: 'The Old Testament is the epos of the Fall of Jerusalem. From the first verse of Genesis to the last of Malachi there rings through it the note of the Capture, the Sack, and the Destruction of the City by the Babylonian Army in 586 B.C. That terrible event is the key to the book. The circumstances which led up to it, the disaster itself, and the consequences which followed, form the subject of the whole.'

[2] Robert Lowth, *Lectures on the Sacred Poetry of the Hebrews* (Boston, 1815), p. 235.

[3] H. Wiesmann, 'Das Leid im Buche der Klagelieder', *Zeitschrift für Aszese und Mystik* 4 (1929), p. 109.

this 'extravagance' of emotion is noticeable to any alert reader. It need not be contested that this is the customary temper of the Semite, but the grief of Lamentations had the deeper significance that from the Hebrew point of view it laments a supreme historical and, therefore, religious catastrophe.

Nearly every strophe of the Book of Lamentations could be cited in proof of the magnitude and severity of the misfortune. In particular the cumulative effect of the strophes in which Yahweh is pictured as chastening his people is overwhelming (1.13-15; 2.1-8; 3.1-19). The purpose of this unrelenting heaping up of misery is to stress the unique nature of the catastrophe, the worst feature being Israel's apparent alienation from God (2.1, 6-7; 3.17, 18, 31, 33, 49, 50; 5.20, 22).

In several passages the uniqueness of the suffering inflicted is actually stated and underlined. To the passers-by the daughter of Zion importunately appeals:

> Is it nothing to you, all you who pass by? Behold and consider
> If there is any pain like my pain, which was dealt to me,
> Which Yahweh inflicted in the day of his fierce anger. (1.12)

This outcry is intended as more than dramatics, although its rhetorical form cannot be denied. Here is a plea for the casual traveller to pause and consider if he has ever beheld such suffering. Perhaps on the grounds of dispassionate reflection alone, forgetting for the moment that it is the despised Zion that suffers, he may have mercy. It is easy to see why Christians have applied this awesome exclamation to the crucifixion of Jesus, for it has a solitariness and anguish akin to that devastating question, 'My God, my God, why hast thou forsaken me?' There is the same piercing quality of irremediable desolation expressed in it.

In the second poem the pivotal strophe is that which follows the withering catalogue of Yahweh's destructive acts:

> How shall I uphold you, with what shall I compare you, O
>   daughter of Jerusalem?
> To what shall I liken you, and how comfort you, virgin
>   daughter of Zion?
> For great as the sea is your ruin; who can heal you? (2.13)

Here the setting has become almost cosmic. Neither heaven nor earth can adduce an analogy to the magnitude of Zion's ruin. It is plainly incalculable. Only the vast, mysterious, and chaotic depths of the sea offer any point of comparison with the extent of Jerusalem's destruction. In the wake of this sweeping pronouncement we are appropriately introduced to the various groups who are inadequate for the comfort and healing of Judah. Neither prophets (2.14), nor the passers-by (2.15), nor the enemy (2.16) are capable of assuaging her wounds. As a matter of fact, like salt rubbed in an open sore, they only intensify the suffering. Failing all human help, the poet urgently summons Zion:

> Cry aloud to the Lord! . . .
> Arise, cry out in the night! . . .
> Lift up your hands to him! . . . (2.18*a*, 19*ae*)

The nadir of Jerusalem's despair has been reached, and the sun of faith begins its circle toward the zenith. Disabused of all illusions, Zion knows that all her trust in earthly deliverance, whether in prophet or king or foreign aid, is ineffectual. The picture of inconsolability in 2.13 is indeed one of the most moving expressions of grief and ruin in all literature and yet it only serves to intensify the need for turning to the Lord. Precisely as in Job, Lamentations gives not the slightest trace of a leaning toward atheism or agnosticism.

Our final example leads logically to the theme of sin but deserves to be discussed in the present context because it boldly links unparalleled suffering with unparalleled sin.

> The iniquity of the daughter of my people is greater than the
>   sin of Sodom;
> She was overthrown in a moment and no hands were laid upon
>   her. (4.6)

The shock of this sort of comparison is apparent. Our poet says in effect: 'Yes, there was one cataclysm which can be compared to Jerusalem's ruin, but, terrible as it was, the fall of Sodom and Gomorrah pales beside the present disaster!'

From the eighth-century prophets onwards, the celebrated Cities of the Plain, Sodom and Gomorrah (cf. Admah and Zeboiim, Gen. 10.19; 14.28), made famous by the vivid J story of Gen. 19, became proverbial for the divine judgment, particu-

larly with respect to its suddenness, its violence and its finality.[1]
It is noteworthy that in all the pre-exilic passages Sodom and its
sister cities are the stock terms for divine judgment on sin. They
serve as the norm for punishment, inasmuch as these cities suffered
the most terrible punishment ever meted out. In each of the
above references the sins of Israel (or the foreign lands) are considered to be perilously like the sins of the wicked cities of
antiquity. But in all these cases Sodom and Gomorrah remain
the standard which the other judgments approximate or equal.
Only in exilic times do we find the sin of the nation *exceeding* that
of the legendary cities! The only analogy to the Lamentations
passage is in the address to the harlot Jerusalem by Ezekiel, who
writes at precisely the same historical juncture:

> And your elder sister in Samaria, who lived with her
> daughters to the north of you; and your younger sister, who
> lived to the south of you, is Sodom with her daughters. Yet
> you were not content to walk in their ways, or do according to
> their abominations; within a very little time you were more
> corrupt than they in all your ways. As I live, says the Lord
> God, your sister Sodom and her daughters have not done as
> you and your daughters have done. (16.46-48)

The special import of the Lamentations reference is that it
reasons from the punishment to the sin in keeping with the most
unerring Deuteronomic faith. In what respect was Zion's
punishment greater than Sodom's? The latter fell by a divine
holocaust from heaven which was presumably instantaneous and
relatively painless for the inhabitants. 'No hands were laid upon
her', but hands *have* been laid upon Jerusalem—the coarse,
plundering, destructive hands of the enemy (cf. 1.7, 10, 14; 2.7;
5.8). So the fitness of the ancient Cities of the Plain as an analogy
to the Fall of Jerusalem is rejected as inadequate. The earlier

---

[1] Richard Kraetzschmar, 'Der Mythus von Sodoms Ende', *ZAW* 17 (1897), pp.
81-92, argues that Gen. 18-19 contain two literary strands, one in which Yahweh
alone is present (singular person) and another where he is represented by three
angels (plural person). The whole myth was originally a Canaanite elohim saga
accounting for the volcanic destruction of the cities (cf. Isa. 34.9). By a long process,
including several editings, it has been appropriated to prophetic Yahwism. But
Kraetzschmar does not touch upon the theological significance of the basic myth
nor allusions to it in subsequent centuries. In fact, among the later passages, he
omits Lam. 4.6.

statements of unparalleled suffering (1.12; 2.13) are emphatically confirmed. A symbol long honoured as the epitome of divinely inflicted punishment is shattered and cast aside. The ruin of Jerusalem, Lamentations insists, defies all categorizing and comparison; it is *sui generis*.

What has brought on the doom? The confession of sin, not once or twice but repeatedly, not perfunctorily or incidentally but earnestly and fundamentally, suggests the reason for the calamity. All five of the poems which comprise the Book of Lamentations witness to the prophetic concept of sin and thus form one link in the long chain of evidence bearing out the importance of Lamentations as a justification and preservation of the teaching of the prophets. Even chapter two, conspicuous in its accusations of the deity, has an awareness of sin. The prophets are at fault because they did not expose the national guilt in order to prevent captivity (2.14). All the frightful judgments might have been averted had the trusted leaders been faithful to their calling and had the sinful people heeded their warning.

The statements of guilt and responsibility for sin are presented in different ways. Sometimes they are found in the poet's description of the city (1.5*d*, 8*a*, 9*a*; 4.6, 13*ab*), sometimes in direct address to the city (2.4*ad*; 4.22*ab*), and then again they appear as confessions on the lips of the city or nation (1.14, 18*ab*, 22*cd*; 3.42; 5.7, 16). The admission of sin by the offender is an absolute necessity if forgiveness is desired. Prov. 28.13, 'He who hides his sins shall not prosper, but he who confesses and forsakes them, shall have mercy,' is a good summary of the Biblical ethos concerning the effectiveness of confessional prayer. In the next chapter we shall explore the character of the repentance which is implied in the very act of acknowledging sin.

With one possible exception the sin is manfully shouldered by the contemporary generation. In 5.7 we read: 'Our fathers sinned and are not; we bear their guilt.' It may be that the 'fathers' are not those of the preceding generations but rather the leaders or eminent among the Jews. In other words, it may be said of the former leaders who are now in captivity that they 'are not', i.e. so far as the Jerusalem community is concerned they have ceased to exist. There is evidence for the usage of אָב, *ābh*, 'father', with respect to rulers, priests, prophets, noblemen (cf. Gen. 45.8;

Judg. 17.10; 18.19; I Sam. 24.11; II Kings 2.12; 3.13; 6.21; 13.14;
II Chron. 2.12). But even if it is to be referred more naturally to
the ancestors, it is not a categorical shifting of responsibility
because in the same poem the people aver: 'The crown has fallen
from our head; woe to us, for we have sinned!' (5.16). From the
Hebrew point of view there is no incompatibility in the entertain-
ing of these two ideas, as indeed the case of Jeremiah so clearly
confirms, not to mention Ezekiel (cf. Jer. 19.12 f with 31.29 and
16.10 ff; also Ezek. 14.21 ff with 18.1 ff). In fact it was the
attempted reconciliation of these two elements of Hebrew experience that was to become one of the major endeavours of Judaism.[1]

First we note that the sin is the equal of the suffering. The sin
which has invoked Jerusalem's downfall is more heinous than
the coarse sensuality of Sodom and Gomorrah (4.6). Twice the
infinitive absolute is used to reinforce the seriousness of the sin
(1.8*a*, 20*d*). Her sin has been so blatant that the nations mock
and desert her (1.5, 8). Her sharp reversal of fortune was solely
because of her sin (1.9). The burden of iniquity was so great
when placed on the back of the daughter of Zion that she was
crushed to the ground (1.14). Her rebellion was so flagrant that
Yahweh was unable to forgive (3.42). The evil of Zion and her
people was as foul as leprosy (4.13-15). There can be no mistake
about the sincerity of the closing summation:

> The crown has fallen from our head; woe to us, for we have
> sinned!
> Because of this our heart is faint, because of these our eyes are
> darkened. (5.16, 17)

As to the specific sins which constitute the great iniquity of
Judah, we are surprised that more detail is not given. It may be
that the incisive teaching of the prophets, contained in the
denunciatory oracles of Amos, Hosea, Isaiah, and Jeremiah, is
here presupposed as the content of the disobedience. Or this may
be a deliberate omission expressive of the poet's conviction that
the sin of Judah was much more serious and deep-rooted than
the combination of many overt acts. This would continue the
interpretation of Jeremiah, who internalized and radicalized sin

---

[1] Justus Köberle, *Sünde und Gnade im religiösen Leben des Volkes Israel bis auf Christum* (München, 1905), p. 277.

to the extent that it could no longer be thought of as simply the violation of commandments imposed from without (cf. esp. 4.14; 13.23; 17.9, 10; 31.33-35).

The one sin that is specified in Lamentations is the irresponsible leadership of the priests and prophets who were remiss in two respects. On the one hand, they were guilty of dereliction of duty in that they delighted in frothy visions of peace and prosperity and failed to warn Judah of her sin and the coming judgment (2.14). On the other hand, they actually participated in the oppression of the righteous, even shedding their blood (4.13). Beyond this the detailed features of the national sin are not sketched. But one thing is sure: the sin is not laid solely at the door of the religious leadership, but is shared equally by the populace. This can be seen in the distinction that is made between the prophet's falsity and 'thy guilt' (2.14). The same is implied, furthermore, in the earnestness of the national confession of guilt and by the fact that, even when priests and prophets have been slain, banished, or carried into exile, the heavy hand of Yahweh's judgment is still upon the community. In fact the gravity of the defection of the religious leaders is only significant in terms of the national destiny and the national default.[1]

The scope and seriousness of the sin is indicated by the several terms employed to describe it[2]: פשע, *peša'*, basically 'transgression, rebellion or infringement', stresses activity (1.5, 14, 22; 3.42); חטא, *ḥēt*, primarily 'failure or falling short', is sin from the standpoint of a norm or formal standard (1.8; 3.39; 4.6, 13, 22; 5.7, 16); עון, *'āwôn*, 'crookedness or straying', is sin from the standpoint of content (2.14; 4.6, 13, 22; 5.7); מרה, *mārāh*, 'obstinacy, refractoriness or rebellion' (1.18, 20; 3.42); and טמאה, *tume'āh*, 'uncleanness' (1.9; 4.15). In this connection it may be significant that שגגה, *šeghāghāh*, 'sin out of ignorance and inadvertence', which does not appear in the prophets, is also avoided in Lamentations, inasmuch as the sin of Judah had long been heralded by the prophets and was therefore inexcusable. It is evident that the several words were used to impress the sin

---

[1] Cf. J. Philip Hyatt, *Prophetic Religion* (Nashville, 1947), pp. 57-60.
[2] The explanation of the Hebrew terminology is derived from Brown, Driver and Briggs, *A Hebrew and English Lexicon of the Old Testament* (Oxford, 1906) and Walter Eichrodt, *Theologie des Alten Testaments* (Berlin, 1950), Teil III, pp. 81 f. Cf. also Pedersen, *Israel* (London, 1926) I-II, p. 414.

upon the hearer and to enable the Judeans to confess whole-heartedly their iniquity before Yahweh.

The confession of sin with such radical vehemence is one of the ways in which our book shows its superiority over all extra-Biblical, and one may also add, over all Biblical laments. Apart from the unusual addendum to the Sumerian Lamentation over Ur,[1] the laments of the ancient Near East known to this writer do not take seriously the connection between national sin and national judgment. This fact testifies eloquently to that deep and sensitive awareness of sin which was the fruition of the prophetic faith of Israel. It demonstrates that sin, both as disobedience and disruption, was understood in exilic Israel. Judaism, with all its defensiveness and exclusivism, developed a deep and interior sense of sin (cf. Ezra 9; Neh. 9; Dan. 9; Sir. 21.1; 39.5; Prayer of Manasseh).[2]

While any such distinction in Lamentations is not articulate (as it is nowhere articulate in the Bible), one senses, both in the transcendent imperious will of the deity and in the tragic broken-ness of the social organism, a wedding of faith and social morality that was to be one of the great gifts of Judaism to the world. The poet in Lamentations shows us that the collective defiance of the word of the Lord (1.18) has resulted in the deepest ruptures of the community life (2.9, 14; 5.1-17). Often in the course of subsequent history there has been a tendency to turn on the one side into an arbitrary tyranny of the divine and on the other into a self-contained ethics. The latter would have been unthinkable for the Hebrews, who knew nothing of autonomous arts, autonomous politics or autonomous culture of any sort. But, the Hebrews, with the possible exception of certain apocalyptists, were not constrained to make of God an arbitrary despot. Unlike the Greek pantheon, Yahweh had the ultimate welfare of his world ever in mind. While for Lamentations, as for all Hebrew thought, there is a definite qualitative chasm between God and man, it nevertheless is true that at the same time man is the child of God and fulfills God's purposes in his historical life. This puts all the

---

[1] James Pritchard, *Ancient Near Eastern Texts Relating to the Old Testament* (Princeton, 1950), pp. 455-463.

[2] Cf. Norman B. Johnson, *Prayer in the Apocrypha and Pseudepigrapha. A Study in the Jewish Concept of God* (Journal of Biblical Literature Monograph Series, Philadelphia, 1948), pp. 24 ff.

'commands' of God in a new perspective and opens up the possibility of talking about natural law, even though the questions of natural law and autonomous ethics do not appear in the Old Testament itself. Nevertheless, the conditions are all there except the humanistic assumption. There is even in the naive faith of the Deuteronomist an expression of the Hebrew conviction that the good of God and good of man are One Good. In this sense Hebrew faith already presupposes and contains, though embryonically, the tensions of later theology. It is not untrue to Biblical faith to raise such rational questions as: Is God or the Good prior? Is an autonomous ethics possible? At least it is not untrue to Biblical faith if it be allowed that the modern religious man may ask religious questions in forms not precisely equivalent to those of the Bible.

The conviction that the nation which lives righteously and trusts God shall be blessed arises out of the fundamental conviction that there are not several goods at conflict with one another but One Good which is the will of Yahweh. Conversely there are not several sins but One Sin which is rebellion against the will of Yahweh. Social ethics, which lay all men under a common obligation, must, therefore, stem from monotheism. It is the given order, created by the One God Yahweh, which rescues the activities of men from sheer arbitrariness and lends them structure. This is why Hebrew religion and Hebrew ethics can never be unravelled to anyone's satisfaction. All rebellion against God is thus not simply rebellion against an 'other' but also against the self and the whole created order, so intimately is the welfare of all created things bound up with adherence to the ways of the creator.[1] One of the great contributions of the Wisdom literature was to make this point articulate. Lam. 3.34-39 is cast against the background of the Creator God, whose ways may be mysterious, but whose purposes are always for the good of his creation. There is, then, one may venture to say, already observable in Lamentations the foundation for the insight that evil and the disintegration of human society are inextricably bound together. There is, in terms of Tillich's philosophical theology,

---

[1] The idea that sin is not simply rebellion against divine fiat but is inimical to human life is implied in much of the prophetic teaching, but it is unusually clear in Hosea's stress upon the knowledge of God as the foundation of social life (cf. 4.1 f, 6, 14; 7.9; 9.7).

71

both an autonomy and a heteronomy within theonomy.[1] The terrible poignancy of the confession of sin in Lamentations is that Zion, by her rebellion, has destroyed herself.

But to attempt to rationalize sin in terms of its social consequences is not to equate the punishment thereof with a troubled conscience, or with the slow working out of requital through the process of moral 'sowing and reaping'. The interventionist ethos of Hebraism is more vivid and direct than that. The Book of Lamentations is distinguished by the repeated emphasis upon the wrath of Yahweh which acts directly in dealing out retribution.[2] Commensurable with the suffering and sin is the anger of Yahweh. The most common term for wrath is אף, *aph*, also 'nostril', a derivative of אנף, *ānaph*, 'breathe or snort' (1.12; 2.1, 3, 21, 22; 3.43, 66; 4.11). Other terms are חרון, *ḥārôn*, from חרה, *ḥārāh*, which has the basic notion of 'burning or kindling' (never alone in Lamentations but three times with אפו, *appô*, 1.12; 2.3; 4.11); חמה, *ḥēmāh*, from יחם, *yāḥam*, with the idea of heat (cf. Aramaic יחם, *yeḥam*, usually for sexual impulse of animals, 2.4; 4.11); עברה, *'ebhrāh*, from עבר, *'ābhar*, which suggests 'over-

---

[1] Paul Tillich, *Systematic Theology* (Chicago, 1951), Vol. 1, pp. 83 ff. As I understand Tillich's discussion of autonomy and heteronomy, the essential point is that ethics is rooted in the created order. On p. 85 he says: 'Autonomy and heteronomy are rooted in theonomy, and each goes astray when their theonomous unity is broken. Theonomy does not mean the acceptance of a divine law imposed on reason by a highest authority; it means autonomous reason united with its own depth. In a theonomous situation reason actualizes itself in obedience to its structural laws and in the power of its own inexhaustible ground. Since God (theos) is the law (nomos) for both the structure and the ground of reason, they are united in him, and their unity is manifest in a theonomous situation.' So far as the Biblical world view was concerned it naturally pictured God as one who commands from without, but it is improper to conceive of his command solely as an arbitrary imposition. This command or Word of God addressed itself to the structural necessity of man. It was directed toward his best interests as when a father issues orders for the good of his son. This is seen at its deepest level in the Old Testament's insistence that the God of Israel and the Creator God are one and the same. Revelation and nature thus have one ultimate source. It seems to me that this drive toward the unification of religious experience would also have a corresponding tendency toward the relating of faith and ethics. Precisely this happened in the Wisdom literature. Thus the increasing cosmogonic reflection of Israel during the exile was not primarily speculative but religio-ethical (cf. Muilenburg, *The Interpreter's Bible*, Vol. I, p. 331).

[2] Otto Procksch, *Theologie des Alten Testaments* (Gütersloh, 1950), pp. 642 f, points out that the anger of Yahweh illustrates the peculiar vitality of the Hebrew view of God. It is in marked contrast to the emphasis of the best Greek minds upon the imperturbable, the 'apathetic' character of God, as witnessed in the classic statement of Aristotle: ἀλλὰ μὴν καὶ ὅτι ἀπαθὲς καὶ ἀναλλοίωτον (*Metaphysics* 1073a). But in the nature of the Hebrew-Jewish God there was something unresting, dynamic, irrational, passionate—all of which is best summarized in the category of the Holy (קדש, *qodheš*).

flow, excess, outburst' (2.2; 3.1); and זַעַם, *za'am*, or 'indignation' (2.6). The verb קָצַף, *qāçaph*, 'to be wrathful' (5.22) completes the vocabulary. Yahweh's wrath is represented as being 'poured out' (הָפַךְ, *hāphakh*, 2.4; 4.11) and as 'accomplished or spent' (כָּלָה, *kālāh*, 4.11). Elsewhere he is pictured as 'wrapping himself in anger' (סָכַךְ, *sākhakh*, 3.43), which like a cloud is impenetrable to prayer (3.44).

The real dynamic of the motif of Yahweh's wrath, however, is lost unless one studies it in close connection with the contexts where it occurs. Only by detailed analysis of the text of Lamentations can the interpreter grasp the fierceness and violence of the divine punishment. Central to the whole matter of the inter-relation of suffering, sin, and wrath is the direct activity of Yahweh in the city's destruction. Sin against God has aroused the divine wrath and that wrath has inflicted punishment without measure or mercy. Lest the reader overlook the true nature of the disaster, the poet ceaselessly reiterates the theme of Yahweh as the relentless, destroying God. Only in the last poem is explicit reference lacking to this motif, but the framework of the chapter, beginning and ending with an appeal for Yahweh to consider and restore the city, as well as the uneasy question of the conclusion, presupposes the earlier belief in the dreadful reprisal of the Lord.

In his monograph on Yahweh as a warrior or military commander, Henning Fredriksson calls attention to the frequent idea of God as the general of foreign armies (cf. e.g. Jer. 50.9; Isa. 41.2, 25; 43.17; Ezek. 26.7; 28.7).[1] Perhaps the most famous expression is that of Assyria as the rod of the divine wrath described by Isaiah of Jerusalem (10.5 ff). From this notion arose the more shocking image of Yahweh himself as the destroyer. In Amos (1.3-2.5) he sends the fire of judgment, not eschatological but simply military (cf. use of the idiom שִׁלַּח בָּאֵשׁ or הִצִּית בָּאֵשׁ, *šālaḥ hiççiṯ—bā'ēš hiççiṯ*, 'to send or kindle fire', in Josh. 8.8, 19; Jud. 1.8; 9.49; 20.48; II Sam. 14.30 f).[2] Yahweh is the one who 'smashes the bars', presumably of the city gates (Amos 1.4 f; Isa. 45.2; Ps. 107.16). But, as Fredriksson observes, the direct destructive work of Yahweh is exemplified in Lamentations

---

[1] Henning Fredriksson, *Jahwe als Krieger. Studien zum alttestamentlichen Gottesbild* (Lund, 1945), pp. 23-27. [2] *Ibid.*, p. 193.

far more baldly than in any other Old Testament book.[1] More ruthless and detailed than even the judgments and punitive messages of the prophets is the inexorable coming of Yahweh as he methodically reduces Zion to ruins. The role of the Divine Punisher is most prominent in four series of strophes; in these passages is concentrated the full impact of the judgment (1.13-15; 2.1-8; 3.1-18, 43-45). The passages may, in turn, be divided into those that represent Yahweh's unmediated action against the nation and those that picture the nation in personified lament.

The second category draws into play the terminology of the individual lament which appears to have been fairly well stylized and rather widely circulated, at least in post-exilic times. Our poet has transferred this imagery of terrible affliction to the nation conceived first, in the form of the daughter of Zion and later, in the person of the prophet Jeremiah. By looking at the verbs descriptive of Yahweh's judgment we get some appreciation of the ferocity and savagery, indeed the vicious glee, with which he carried out his plan. The general term for the punishment inflicted is יגה, *yāghāh*, 'to afflict' (1.5, 12) but it is embellished by imagery declaring that Yahweh cast fire into her bones, stretched a net to entangle her feet (1.13), impressed a yoke of sin upon her (1.14), spurned her warriors, summoned a festival of slaughter and trod the bloody 'winepress' (1.15).

Yet the first chapter is only a foretaste of what appears in the third poem where the severity of the divine punishment mounts almost to the breaking point. The suffering man depicted is the prophet Jeremiah as a type or representative of the suffering nation; his chastisements are administered by the rod of Yahweh's wrath (שבט עברת, *šēbheṭ ‘ebhrāthô*). But the initial announcement of the lamenting figure is an understatement of the fury to come. In rapid succession Yahweh drives him into darkness (3.2), turns a continually hostile hand against him (3.3), wears away his bodily strength and substance (3.4), besieges him (3.5), makes him dwell in the darkness of death (3.6), walls off his path with stones (3.7, 9), burdens him with chains (3.7), ignores his prayer (3.8), ambushes and tears him like a wild beast (3.10, 11), pierces him with arrows (3.12, 13), sates him with poisonous food and drink (3.15), breaks his teeth (3.16) and forces him to cower in

[1] *Loc. cit.*

ashes (3.16). It is no wonder that the man cries out in despair:

Thou hast rejected me from peace; I have forgotten good,
So I say, 'Gone is my endurance, my hope from Yahweh.'

(3.17, 18)

When we remember the historic circumstances which underlie the extravagance of the third chapter, the imagery does not appear unreasonable. Jeremiah's rejection by his countrymen was, to all appearances, the most complete which any prophet ever experienced, at least that rejection is most sensitively preserved in his writings. As to the destruction of Judah, we have already noted that never had the city of Jerusalem and the kingdom at large known such a total and humiliating defeat. While the descriptions are excessive to our Western canons of taste, they are not disproportionate to the suffering as the people of Judah, the prophet Jeremiah, and the poet had experienced it. It is important to remember that to the Israelite what we speak of as 'the fall of Jerusalem' was not a single instantaneous stroke but an agonizing succession of blows, a tragedy compounded of many tragedies, a lingering and excruciating pain persisting in the form of shame and reproach long after the first distresses of the siege and destruction had subsided.

For the more explicit development of the destructive fury of Yahweh, we must turn to the remaining group of passages where the divine initiative is so to the fore that the instrumentality of the judgment, namely, the Neo-Babylonians, vanishes from sight and the grim demolition of Jerusalem is carried out by God himself. This is definitely more than a poetic device; indeed, mere aesthetics would recoil from such a perverse image. It can only be understood as a calculated attempt to attribute each and every one of Zion's tragic misfortunes to the will of Yahweh. Thus the secondary cause recedes and the will which originated the destruction is pictured as executing it. *He* (Yahweh) has beclouded the daughter of Zion, cast her glory from heaven to earth, disregarded his footstool (2.1), destroyed the dwellings of Jacob, thrown down the fortifications, hurled king and princes to the ground (2.2), cut off Israel's strength, turned back Israel's hand before the enemy, burned in Jacob as a flaming fire (2.3), bent his bow, set his hand and slain her sons (2.4), become as an enemy, destroyed her palace and fortifications, multiplied mourning and moaning (2.5), pulled down his booth and assembly place, caused festival and Sabbath to be forgotten, spurned king and priest (2.6), rejected altar and sanctuary, measured off the walls for destruction (2.7), and caused wall and rampart to mourn (2.8).

Later in the same poem Zion addresses Yahweh on behalf of her slaughtered inhabitants:

> Thou hast slain in the day of thine anger; thou hast slaughtered without mercy.
> Thou hast called as a day of festival sojourners from round about,
> And in the day of Yahweh's anger there is neither refugee nor survivor. (2.21*e*-22*d*)

There is also a relevant passage in the third poem where the nation, in a mixture of amazement and self-reprehension, directs a prayer of protest to the Lord:

> Thou hast clothed thyself with anger and pursued, thou hast slain and had no mercy;
> Thou hast clothed thyself in a cloud, prayer is unable to pass through.
> Offscouring and refuse thou hast made us in the midst of the peoples. (3.43-54)

Elsewhere the mocking enmity of surrounding peoples is openly attributed to Yahweh's decree (1.17). He caused the enemy to rejoice and actually exalted the strength of the foe (2.17), and he has scattered the faithless prophets and priests with his fierce countenance (4.16).

Nowhere in the five poems do we discover any mitigation of the inexorable and pitiless performance of God in the city's overthrow. To be sure other very important and hope-producing aspects of the deity are presented, but the calamity proper is consistently pictured as *planned* and *executed* by Yahweh. Even when the ruthless enemy is the centre of attention it is taken for granted that he is the momentary instrument of God, for 'He (Yahweh) has delivered into the hands of the enemy the walls of her palaces' (2.7) and 'The Lord gave me into the hands of those whom I cannot withstand' (1.14). One suspects that the repeated insistence upon this point is the poet's way of impressing his conviction on the wavering and doubtful in Judah. How widely the proposition was shared among the Jews remaining in Palestine is difficult to estimate, but in Lamentations it is clearly axiomatic. No accident, no demon, no foreign god was responsible for the plight of Israel, but Yahweh alone. In fact this becomes the basis of the enemy's cruellest scorn: the god who, by your own definition, should have protected you, has destroyed you!

> Listen when I groan! There is none to comfort me;
> All my enemies rejoice over my fate that thou hast done it!
>   (1.21)

And still more emphatic is the announcement that

> Yahweh has done what he purposed; he has accomplished his threat
> Which he decreed from days of old; he has pulled down without mercy,
> And caused the enemy to rejoice over you; he has exalted the strength of your enemies. (2.17)

Next to the loss of community with Yahweh and his purposes, the bitterest aspect of doom is the shame and reproach of defeat. The shame of Jerusalem consists primarily in her weakness so that she is unable to stand against the onslaughts of the foe (1.7-10; 2.16). She utterly failed to live up to her self-styled image as the city honoured (1.1*e*, 8*c*). As a consequence of the devastating blow which befell her, the nation is overcome with shame. Her disgrace is seen in two directions. In the first place she is swept by revulsion because of her sins (1.8). The daughter of Zion appears in the shocking image of a brazen harlot whose filthiness is publicly known. The force of the word 'filthy' (נידה, *nîdhāh*) can be seen in its technical usage for a menstruating woman (Ezek. 18.6; 22.10; 36.17; Lev. 12.2; 15.19, 20; 24-26; 18.19). By her callous persistence in sin, the daughter of Zion has so defiled herself that she is a thing of utter abhorrence to herself and others and in her revulsion she 'turns away' from the gaze of her former lovers (1.8, 9, 17).

In a similar manner the figure of leprosy is used to communi-

cate the horrible aversion felt toward the faithless persons who
held positions of religious leadership. The garments of priests
and prophets are polluted and the community expels them from
its midst with the warning cry of the leper: 'Unclean! Unclean!'
(4.13-15). Jerusalem's sin, then, is like a foul and infectious disease that continually contaminates the daughter of Zion, exposing
her to the open contempt and ostracism of the larger Near
Eastern community. But in a more limited sense, those especially
guilty within the nation, the priests and prophets, are doubly
infected and bear a particular scorn and ignominy.

The cruellest shame borne by Zion is the reproach of the enemy
and neighbour who delight in mockery and revel in the punishment of Israel. The sharpest sting of Judah's sinfulness is the
fact that it has been uncovered to the curious and hateful view of
former friends. 'All her admirers despise her, for they have seen
her nakedness' (עֶרְוָתָהּ, *'erwāthāh*, 1.8, is another word of
offence, actually a euphemism for the pudenda, cf. Gen. 9.22, 23;
Ezek. 16.37; 23.10, 29; Isa. 20.4; 47.3). And it is evident from
4.21, 22 that the identical shameful exposure of Edom is anticipated, when her sins will be bared to the castigating derision of
all the nations, for 'you shall become drunk and strip yourself
bare . . . he [Yahweh] will uncover your sins.'

It was observed in the previous chapter that there is a frequent
contrast in the Book of Lamentations between Judah's fall and
the enemy's rise. This reversal of fortune is inextricably bound
up with a sense of bitter reproach:

> Her enemies have gained the ascendancy, her foes have
>   triumphed. (1.5*ab*)
> The enemies see her; they laugh at her annihilation. (1.7*gh*)
> So that her fall is awesome, with none to comfort her.
> Behold, O Yahweh, my affliction, for the enemy magnifies
>   himself! (1.9*c-f*)
> Behold, O Yahweh, and consider, for I am despised! (1.11*ef*)
> All my enemies rejoice over my evil that thou hast done it.
>   (1.21*cd*)

So odious has Judah become that in one passage she declares that
Yahweh has made her like garbage or manure (מָאוֹס, *mā'ôs*,
'what has been rejected'; סְחִי, *seḥî*, 'what has been scraped off or

cleared away', cf. Ezek. 26.4 and the Talmudic, סחותא, *seḥûthā,* 'refuse' and the Targumic סחיתא, *seḥîthā,* 'dirt, dung').

Other verses tell of the nations directing taunt songs against the desolated city:

> He has made me a laughing-stock to all my people, their song of derision all the day. (3.14)
>
> All our enemies open their mouth at us. (3.46)
>
> Thou hast heard their taunts, O Yahweh, all their plans against me,
>
> The lips of my assailants and their thoughts against me all the day;
>
> Behold their sitting and their rising! For I am their song of derision! (3.61-63)

The taunt or mocking song must have been a firmly established Semitic genre. One of the earliest fragments of Hebrew poetry preserves just such a derisive song against Heshbon (Num. 21.27-29). Two later taunt songs, though polished by literary finesse and reshaped by prophetic ideas, are instructive for our understanding of the type (Isa. 14, 47). But we are still more fortunate in having retained in the text of Lamentations what appear to be some of the phrases and refrains from the typical exilic taunt song. We cannot know whether they record the actual words that were hurled at Judah by certain of the enemy but it is enough if they retain the spirit. Accompanied as they are by gestures, malicious joy and hateful malignancy, the sharp whiplash of their scorn is not lost to the modern interpreter:

> All who pass by clap their hands at you;
>
> They hiss and shake their heads at the daughter of Jerusalem;
>
> "Is this the city of which they said 'perfect in beauty, the joy of all the earth'?"
>
> All your enemies open their mouth at you;
>
> They hiss and gnash their teeth, they say, 'We have destroyed her!'
>
> 'Surely this is the day for which we waited. It is ours! We see it!' (2.15, 16)

It is interesting that in Isa. 14 and 23 we have the same ironic type of question as in 2.15, questions calculated to stress the great chasm between former pretension and present weakness and humiliation. The former accomplishes by means of dramatic contrast very nearly the same effect as Shelley achieved in his sonnet 'Ozymandias'.

> Those who see you will stare at you,
>   and ponder over you:
> 'Is this the man who made the earth tremble,
>   who shook kingdoms,
> Who made the world like a desert
>   and overthrew its cities,
>   who did not let the prisoners go home?' (Isa. 14.16, 17)
>
> 'Is this your exultant city
>   whose origin is from days of old,
> whose feet carried her
>   to settle afar?' (Isa. 23.7)

The very fact that the greatest shame revealed in the poems is not the personal shame of sin but the public shame of reproach poses the crucial theological issue of a universal God confining himself to a particular people. The light that has fallen on Israel has been gravely refracted, for Israel has all too often understood her Lord as the protector of her national interests and, conversely, she has tended to define God's enemies in terms of her own enemies. From the standpoint of Christianity, and also in the opinion of many adherents of Judaism, a shattering of the theocracy was necessary in order to release the word of God from its too narrow and too selfish confines.

But even in its post-exilic form, Judaism did not become a world religion in actuality. This must be insisted upon in spite of widespread geographical dispersion and, for a period at least, a thriving proselyte movement.[1] The loftiest sentiments of universalism did not set aside the plain fact that to share the religion of the One God Yahweh meant that one must become a Jew culturally. There can be little doubt that the rise of Christianity shut the door on whatever hope there might have been for a truly universal Judaism, or perhaps one ought to say that the universalistic tendencies in Judaism found their expression in the daughter religion of Christianity. At any rate, it appears that

[1] Cf. Bernard Bamberger, *Proselytism in the Talmudic Period* (Cincinnati, 1939) and his article in *The Universal Jewish Encyclopedia*, Vol. 9, pp. 1-3.

only the one 'branch' of Hebrew-Jewish faith, namely Christianity, succeeded in overcoming the connection between faith and nationality. In the very process of doing so it became heretical to the parent faith. It is true that Christianity retained an offence, but in place of the offence of nationality, it placed the offence of the cross (and the related offence of the incarnation).[1] While both were scandals of particularity, the Christian offence was able to cut radically across all levels of society, culture and race—something which Judaism has never quite succeeded in doing. Christ was and is a scandal to the proud man *as man*; Judaism was and is a scandal to the gentile *as gentile*. Christianity therefore realizes all that is best in the historical faith of Hebraism and Judaism but, in addition, lifts this faith to a level where it is accessible to men everywhere, without demanding of them extraneous cultural and ritual submission. This is typified in the fact that Jesus utterly transformed a Jewish title of limited national meaning into a term of universal significance. If it is true that Hebrew faith gives us the necessary understanding of the term *Christ*, it is also true that Jesus invested the title with its decisive content—a content that could never have been predicted or inferred from its Old Testament antecedents.[2] When the Church calls itself 'the New Israel' this simply means that Christians believe themselves to be participating in the promises of God which were not alone *to* Israel but *through* Israel to all the world.

In this criticism of Jewish pride, we do not mean that an insensitivity to the reproach of the enemy and the onlooker would have been the ideal attitude for the poet of Lamentations. Without this sting the lament would have been plainly insipid! Furthermore, this sensitivity shows a recognition that all the brutality and cruelty of the foe could not be equated solely with Yahweh's will. Although an instrument in Yahweh's hand, the enemy was not passive. Its wilfulness became apparent in delight over the havoc which it wrought. Nevertheless the fact persists that the great indulgence of Lamentations in the reproach of the

[1] A superb discussion of the scandal of the cross can be found in Paul Minear, *Eyes of Faith* (Philadelphia, 1946), pp. 270 f.
[2] This concentration of originally independent titles and expectations in Jesus of Nazareth so that, in effect, he remakes the categories, is thoroughly depicted in William Manson, *Jesus the Messiah* (Philadelphia, 1946).

F

enemy is a blemish of national pride not suited to the mission of Israel. Wiesmann argues that by virtue of Israel's uniqueness as the people of revelation, she was 'marked' as the special target of scorn by the surrounding nations. Because of her privileges and peculiarities, Israel was easily incited to pride and nothing would be more rancorous in the breast of surrounding peoples than such superiority.[1] The destruction of Jerusalem should have taught the Jew not only humility toward Yahweh but a greater charity toward the non-Jew. While the distinction has been very hard for men to make, especially religious men, there is a difference between suffering for the sake of one's faith and suffering because of recalcitrance and stubborn pride. It is hard to avoid the conclusion that in the very superbness of Hebraism with its privileges and excellencies there was a perverseness of pride which God had to judge—a perverseness which is not absent from the Christian Church or indeed from any organization or nation that has some basis for self-satisfaction.

Precisely as in the prophets, Lamentations does not totally renounce the election doctrine of Israel. In spite of that, by means of the enormity of her sin and the exhortation to patience and a wider trust in the overarching and mysterious ways of God, a number of reservations are introduced into the optimistic formulations of the election faith. Not only is responsibility primary, but there is some indication that Yahweh's purposes are too grand and unpredictable to be limited to one people. From the following in Lamentations it is only a short step to the great statements of universalism in Second Isaiah:

> Who is this who speaks and it is so, unless the Lord commands?
> From the mouth of the Most High has there not gone forth
>   evil and good?
> Why should a living man murmur, a man because of his sins?
>   (3.37-39)

In our consideration of the theology of doom in Lamentations, we turn finally to the motif of the Day of Yahweh[2] (יום יהוה,

---

[1] Wiesmann, *op. cit.*, p. 108.

[2] The origin and import of the Day of Yahweh has been the subject of intense and protracted debate. The two classic works are Hugo Gressmann, *Der Ursprung der israelitischen-jüdischen Eschatologie* (Göttingen, 1905), pp. 141-158, and Sigmund Mowinckel, *Psalmenstudien II. Das Thronbesteigungsfest Jahwäs und der Ursprung der*

yôm yhwh) which forms another link between our book and the prophets. All discussion of the Day of Yahweh begins with Amos who clearly shows that the concept as popularly held in his day was a creation of quasi-religious patriotism (5.18). His comprehension was quite otherwise, for he envisioned stern judgment on gentile and Israelite alike. It is this view of a radical 'root and branch' destruction of evil, regardless of national boundaries, that is perpetuated and restated by a long succession of prophets (Isa. 2.12; Zeph. 1.10-12; Ezek. 7.10; Joel 1.14; Mal. 4.1).[1]

When we examine Lamentations we are impressed with the extent to which it bears out this prophetic conviction. In no sense is its conception of the Day of Yahweh related to the popular idea reflected in Amos. There are several references to the Day of Yahweh, although in only one does the usual name appear and this may be a gloss (2.22). But the features of that day accord with the prophetic teaching:

> Is it nothing to you, all you who pass by? Behold and consider
> If there is any pain like my pain which was dealt to me,
> Which Yahweh inflicted *in the day of his fierce anger*.
>
> (1.12, ביום חרון אפו, *běyôm ḥărôn appô*)

> O how the Lord has eclipsed in his anger the daughter of Zion!
> Has cast from heaven to earth the glory of Israel!
> And has taken no thought of his footstool *in the day of his anger*!
>
> (2.1, ביום אפו, *běyôm appô*)

Eschatologie (Kristiana, 1922). The most searching recent criticisms of their theories are well summarized in Stanley Frost, *Old Testament Apocalyptic. Its Origins and Growth* (London, 1952), pp. 39 ff, and H. W. Robinson, *Inspiration and Revelation in the Old Testament* (Oxford, 1946), pp. 139 ff. Perhaps the most satisfactory line of approach is that taken by J. M. P. Smith, 'The Day of Yahweh', *American Journal of Theology* 5 (1901), pp. 505-533, who stresses the uniqueness of Israelite eschatology as the ancillary of the historical faith in Yahweh. He sees the roots of the conception as early as the Yahwist epic. The most exhaustive recent treatment is that of Ladislav Černý, *The Day of Yahweh and Some Relevant Problems* (Prague, 1948) who strongly accents the social and historical factors which shaped the development of Hebrew eschatology. When pressed to state wherein the uniqueness of the latter may be found he is driven to affirm that 'it is only this idea of the necessity of change in the existing world which makes the conception of the Day of Yahweh unique among the Hebrews' (p. 98).

[1] It is worth noting, however, that the Day of Yahweh, or at least the term, does not appear in Hosea, Micah or Habakkuk. The reason for this omission may well have been a desire to avoid any misunderstanding on the part of the people who, hearing mention of the Day of Yahweh, would have misconstrued it in the nationalistic sense (J. M. P. Smith, *op. cit.*, p. 515).

Young and old lie prostrate in the streets;
My maidens and young men fall by the sword;
Thou hast slain *in the day of thine anger*; thou hast slaughtered
without mercy. (2.21, ביום אפך, *běyôm appekhā*)

Thou hast called as a day of festival sojourners from round
about,
And *in the day of Yahweh's anger* there is neither refugee nor survivor;
Those whom I fondled and reared my enemy consumed.
(2.22, ביום אף-יהוה, *běyôm aph-yhwh*)

Of immediate interest in these passages is the identification of
the Day of Yahweh with the fall of Jerusalem in confirmation of
the prophets' firm faith that it was to be a day of doom for Israel.
As Černý observes, the designation of the Day of Yahweh as *past*
is absolutely unique to the Book of Lamentations.[1] The significance of this fact must not be overlooked. First, it shows the
decisive and epochal nature of the fall of the city. If was of such
world-shaking import for Israel that it could be described as the
Day of Yahweh. This confirms the many other indications of
the *sui generis* nature of the catastrophe. Secondly, it should be
abundantly clear that Day of Yahweh in our period, at least for
the poet of Lamentations, could scarcely have been regarded as
the culmination of history, i.e. the point at which history ends
in one great act of God. If it had been so regarded, it would have
been impossible to equate the fall of the city, however calamitous,
with that Day, for it was obvious that history was still in process.
Finally, it clarifies for the exegete the basic connotation of the
Day of Yahweh. We shall see momentarily that Lamentations
not only regards the Day of Yahweh as past but also conceives
of it as future (1.21). Were the Day a given period of time con-
sisting of twenty-four hours, or even a single event, such a
bifurcation would be ridiculous. But the Day of Yahweh is not
any stated period of time.[2] Temporality is involved only in the
sense that Yahweh will act openly in history. Thus it is Yahweh's
'Day' because it is *the time when God acts*. 'Day' is simply that
portion of history in which God moves decisively to judge men
and to fulfill his purposes. Lamentations is thereby able to
represent two or more times as the Day of Yahweh, corresponding

[1] Černý, *op. cit.*, p. 20.   [2] *Ibid.*, Chap. I.

to the twofold character of his judgment: once upon Israel in the past and again upon the enemy nations in the future. Both of these are Yahweh's Day without any sense of inconsistency. Lamentations is unique in this double reference for the Day of Yahweh. It can only be explained in the light of the enormity of the impression made by the fall of the city.

If the Day of Yahweh is essentially the period of time in which Yahweh acts (cf. Mal. 3.17), what is the character of his action? Our book is uniform in its witness that the action of God is the expression of his wrath (cf. Isa. 13.6, 9; Zeph. 1.18; 2.2 f; 3.9 f; Ezek. 7.19). In fact the accepted expression in Lamentations is 'the Day of his anger'. We have already seen how the intense wrath of Yahweh is pictured as afflicting, annihilating, and profaning the city of Jerusalem, its citizens and holy places.

Among the imagery in which the Day of Yahweh is decked out, the most prominent is the *battle-motif*. Yahweh appears as a slaying warrior (2.4, 5, 21; 3.43), drenched in the 'vintage' blood of his victims (1.15), burning (1.13; 2.3-4; 4.11) and demolishing (2.2, 5-6) the city. Some of this imagery has a demonic coloration, attributing to Yahweh functions once cared for by the lesser divinities who intervened capriciously in the affairs of men (cf. Gen. 32.22 ff). Fredriksson singles out for consideration the blazing face of Yahweh which destroys and scatters, a tradition going back to the numinous Sinai experience when it was said that no man could look upon Yahweh's face and live (Ex. 34.29 ff).[1] It is the hostile face of Yahweh that dissipates the faithless leaders (4.16). Yahweh as an archer whose arrows cause sickness and misfortune takes over that function from demonology (3.2 f cf. Job 6.4; 16.12 f; Deut. 32.22; Ps. 38.3; 64.8).[2] We have noted the starkness of the imagery of God's punishment and also the extent to which the secondary cause (the enemy) is overlooked and the primary cause (Yahweh) is emphasized. S. R. Driver remarks that this habit is typical of the Day of Yahweh theme: 'The conception places out of sight the human agents, by whom actually the judgment, as a rule, is effected, and regards the decisive movements of history as the exclusive manifestation of Jehovah's purpose and power.'[3]

[1] Fredriksson, *op. cit.*, p. 90.   [2] *Ibid.*, p. 95.
[3] S. R. Driver, *Joel and Amos*. The Cambridge Bible (Cambridge, 1901), p. 185.

The *darkness-motif* of Amos (cf. Isa. 13.9 f; Joel 2.2, 10 f; Ezek. 30.3) is not so explicit in Lamentations. The image of Zion as a star eclipsed by the wrath of Yahweh may be an instance (2.1). But unrecognized by most commentators is the *sacrifice-motif* in the reference 'as to a day of appointed festival' (2.22). This ironic word makes explicit and understandable one feature of the Day of Yahweh that appears for the first time in Zephaniah:

Be silent before the Lord God!
   For the day of the Lord is at hand;
the Lord has prepared a sacrifice
         and consecrated his guests.
And on the day of the Lord's sacrifice—
   'I will punish the official and the king's sons
   and all who array themselves in foreign attire.' (1.7 f)

It is also found prior to Lamentations in Jer. 46.10[1]:

That day is the day of the Lord God of hosts,
   a day of vengeance,
   to avenge himself on his foes.
The sword shall devour and be sated,
   and drink its fill of their blood.
For the Lord God of hosts holds a sacrifice
   in the north country by the river Euphrates.

In exilic times and thereafter the sacrifice was developed into the great eschatological feast (cf. Isa. 34.5-7; Ezek. 39.4, 17-20; Pseudo-Isaiah 25.6-8; I Enoch 62.14; II Esdras 6.52; II Baruch 29.4; Luke 14.15-24; Matt. 7.11; 22.2-14).[2] The figure originated perhaps in the popular patriotic idea that the Day of Yahweh was to be a day of joyful deliverance, a truly festal occasion.[3] If the anticipated day was an outgrowth of the cult then the idea of the festival of Yahweh would be all the more understandable.[4] The difficulty is, of course, that each of the facets of the Day of Yahweh permits of the same kind of provincial interpretation.

[1] The oracle in Jeremiah 46 concerning the Battle of Carchemish is attributed to the prophet of Anathoth by nearly all commentators.
[2] Excellent discussions of the eschatological feast in its various developments are found in Frost, *op. cit.*, pp. 52, 90, 152 f; Gressmann, *op. cit.*, pp. 136-141; Mowinckel, *op. cit.*, pp. 296 f.
[3] Cf. Georg Hoffmann, 'Versuche zu Amos', *ZAW* 3 (1883), p. 112.
[4] Mowinckel's forte is in the cultic interpretation.

The battle imagery suggests a military origin.[1] The nature imagery suggests a cosmic setting supplied by myth or eschatology.[2] The truth may be that military, cosmic, and cultic imagery was employed to give colour to a conception that was derived from none of these supposed 'sources'.

The ironic twist that the prophets gave to the *sacrifice-motif* was strictly for the purpose of lending force to their persuasion that judgment would begin with God's people. 'Yes,' agrees the grieving poet, 'we came as those who are summoned to a festival. We crowded Jerusalem in anticipation of victory over the Babylonians but on Yahweh's Day none of us escaped. The sword was turned against us and instead of feasting we were feasted upon!' The mention of cannibalism in the context carries overtones of sadism and brutality that underline the demonic spectacle.[3] It is also possible that in the third poem the statements 'he has driven me into darkness and not light' (3.2 cf. Amos 5.18c, 20) and 'like a bear he ambushed me, like a lion in hiding' (3.10 cf. Amos 5.19ab) are employed with the thought that the appalling suffering here inflicted is the Day of Yahweh now realized as Amos predicted it.

Ordinarily commentators discuss the last two strophes of the second poem simply as an instance of unbridled vengefulness. Vengeance is not to be excluded, but, in addition, we find here a crucial reference to the Day of Yahweh as a day of visitation on the nations:

Listen when I groan! There is none to comfort me;
All my enemies rejoice over my fate that thou hast done it;
Bring to pass *the day thou didst proclaim* when they shall be as I!

Bring all their evil before thee! and do with them
As thou hast done with me, because of all my sins.
For great are my groanings and my heart is faint. (1.21, 22)

---

[1] W. R. Smith, *The Prophets of Israel* (London, 1897), pp. 397 f, argues that the Day of Yahweh originated as a Day of Battle.

[2] W. Cossmann, *Die Entwicklung des Gerichtsgedankens bei dem alttestamentlichen Propheten*. Beihefte zur Zeitschrift für die alttestamentliche Wissenschaft 29 (1915), pp. 178 ff, maintains that the Day of Yahweh was originally a term for Yahweh's revelation, devoid of any judgment associations, as the nature imagery clearly shows.

[3] Although no direct connection is likely, Černý points to an Assyrian text associating cannibalism with the future judgment. It is predicted that in the reign of a certain prince 'the brother will eat his brother' and 'the people will sell their children for money' (p. 64).

Pedersen remarks that in spite of the protest of Amos, many of the later prophets fostered the view that God would one day smite the foes of Israel and reign over his people as King (cf. Zeph. 3.18, 15; Obad. 15, 21; Isa. 27; 33-35; 52; Ezek. 38.9; Zech. 14; Joel 2.28-3.20).[1] In this spirit the poet of Lamentations believed not only that there is a Day of Yahweh for Israel but also a Day of Yahweh for the foe 'when they shall be as I', i.e. when their evils are dealt with. And this is no afterthought in the divine plan but a Day long 'announced' by Yahweh (1.21, קרא, *qārā*). Here is something more than mere vengeance; it is the protest of outraged injustice.[2] It is not denied, or in any way excluded, that the fall of the city was a bona fide judgment of Yahweh, but it is felt that the chastisement of Judah did not fully rectify the injustices of history. There is an increment of judgment yet to come.

That all is not complete with Yahweh's administration of justice is evident in the mockery and glee of the foe. The punishment of Israel did not cure all evil; indeed, it gave opportunity for the lust and vicious traits of the enemy to be indulged (1.21; 2.7, 15, 16; 3.59-63; 4.18, 21; 5.5, 11, 12). Thus we have the germ of the universal judgment when at the Great Assize God will review the evil of all men and reward them as he has prematurely rewarded Israel. Such an outlook is not contradictory to Amos, for the reverse side of the herdsman's teaching about God's universal rule (9.7) was the conviction that the Universal Ruler would hold these nations responsible for their wrongs (1.3-2.3). Given the changed situation of the exile, it was inevitable that this other side of the doctrine would be developed.

The destructive or 'demonic' character of Yahweh was an

---

[1] Pedersen, *op. cit.*, III-IV, p. 546.

[2] Paul Heinisch, *Theology of the Old Testament* (Collegeville, Minnesota, 1950), p. 201, defends certain of the Old Testament expressions of hostility as follows: '. . . every violent word reflects the consciousness of intimate union with God and a living faith in His justice. The hatred of the pious, whose sentiments the Old Testament hands down to us, is directed primarily against sin, and thereby is elevated above a merely personal or natural spirit of revenge.' H. G. Mitchell, *The Ethics of the Old Testament* (Chicago, 1912), p. 235, emphasizes the same point: 'Insofar as the instruments that Yahweh has chosen have gone beyond his instructions, they are guilty and must in their turn pay the penalty of their presumption.' Commenting on our book he says: 'The moral tone of the book comes out most strongly in Lam. 4.22, where the author announces to Zion the termination of her suffering, and to Edom the approach of a similar visitation, because the former has satisfied the demands of the divine justice while the latter has not yet atoned for her offences.'

apprehension of the deity which Hebraism never surrendered. It is crucial, nevertheless, to recognize the way in which pure caprice and arbitrariness were subordinated by the prophets to the righteous purposes of the Most High. In the next chapter we shall have more to say about this 'ethicizing' of the demonic. What is unique in Lamentations is the author's fearlessness in boldly asserting the explosive and destructive side of the divine nature. What is of importance is not merely the tremendous power and energy of Yahweh which can destroy the proudest works of man. That which is of enduring significance is the determination and ability of Yahweh to act in history in fulfilment of his announced word. The doom that he has brought upon Judah is not the result of fitful moodiness but is in accordance with the long proclaimed and inevitable requital of disobedience and rebellion. The Book of Lamentations was the first to take up the prophets' theme in the wake of the tragedy they announced and to vindicate their claims.

The consequence of this acceptance of the prophetic interpretation of national tragedy was immense. It deserves to be regarded as the greatest single spiritual achievement of the exile. The continuation of Hebrew religion depended upon it, for the survival of Israel's faith was predicated on the existence of at least a nucleus of believers who would be disposed to heed the words of men like Ezekiel and Deutero-Isaiah. Lamentations, originating on the home soil of Palestine, addressed to the people and intended for popular consumption, lays bare the heart of the process by which despair was turned to faith and disillusion to hope. In the attributing of the destruction and disorder of the nation to the divine will, strange as it may seem, we may discern the roots of new life. Calamity in itself might profit nothing. Humanly speaking, everything depended on a substantial number of Israelites recognizing the chastening hand of God at work in the unhappy events. Only in this way could history become revelatory with the purposes of God. Following 586 B.C. historical religion wavered perilously between collapse and reaffirmation. What was demanded in a great act of faith was the acceptance of the doom as Yahweh's doing, in large measure attributable to Israel's sins, but even in its incomprehensibility and mystery, still wholly within the designs of God.

CHAPTER FIVE

THE THEOLOGY OF HOPE

Not many years ago the very mention of a message of hope would have been enough to demonstrate beyond the shadow of a doubt that such a message did not originate with the prophets. There was an ironclad 'law' of prophecy which forbade the spokesman of Yahweh ever to hold forth promises or to offer consolation. At least this was the case with the pre-exilic prophets, and, to the degree that certain exilic and post-exilic prophets departed from the word of absolute doom, to that degree they were thought of as forsaking the rigorous prophetic heights and compromising their mission by concessions to the feelings of the people at large.

But all this is changed. It is now widely recognized that the prophet was no mere automaton who had only one thing to say and only one way of saying it, like a record endlessly repeated. A study of the prophets only increases our amazement at their individuality and adaptability in the face of changing circumstances. To cut out all elements of hope from the prophecies of Hosea, Isaiah, and Jeremiah calls for such wholesale surgery on the text and does such violence to the psychology of the prophets themselves, that the pursuit, if not wholly abandoned, is now tempered with much greater caution and reserve.

This is not to say that every passage of hope in the pre-exilic prophets is genuine.[1] Each one must be tested on its own merits and, to a great extent, the negative judgments of previous critics are to be maintained. What must be decried is their doctrinaire presumption which allowed, or even forced, them to reject passages on principle. Even so historically exacting a critic as T. J. Meek has pointed to the likelihood of a prophetic message of hope inasmuch as the combination of threat and promise can be detected in Egyptian writings as early as the Twelfth Dynasty (2000-1800 B.C.).[2]

We have, however, not only the evidence of the writings them-

---

[1] J. Philip Hyatt, *Prophetic Religion* (Nashville, 1947), pp. 96-108 suggests useful criteria for determining authentic passages of hope.

[2] T. J. Meek, *Hebrew Origins* (New York, 1950 rev. ed.), p. 181.

selves and the probabilities suggested by Egyptian parallels, but we have the historical survival of prophetic religion. Had the prophets preached destruction only, and held forth no glimmer of hope beyond tragedy, it is difficult to understand how Yahwism could have survived. Again and again students of the Old Testament have observed that Israel affords an amazing exception to the ancient Near Eastern pattern; Hebrew faith did not decline with national adversity but actually was confirmed and deepened. This was in large measure due to the prophetic conviction about chastisement, repentance, conversion, and hope. Martin Noth has given apt expression to the present tendency in prophetic interpretation[1]:

> Amid the destructive events of the eighth and seventh centuries the prophets had not only spoken the threatening word as immanent and events as containing the judgment of God, but at the same time on occasion they spoke a word about God's further plans with Israel.

With this in mind, then, it will not seem strange or impossible that Lamentations, in its declaration of hope, is taking up a prophetic strain of thought and giving it that development and emphasis which could only have been possible after the predicted calamity had fallen. Specifically, the theology of hope in the Book of Lamentations is not a finely wrought description of future glory in the apocalyptic style. It is, rather, the intimation of a bright future which is determined by the nature of Israel's God. This rules out all speculative indulgence about the precise character of the future. On the contrary, this 'theology of hope' concentrates upon the revealed character of the God who determines the future and upon that response which is required of Israel if she is to participate in God's future.

We may begin our tracing of this hope by noting the frequency with which prayer appears in our book. The several imperatives directed to God are of theological importance inasmuch as they show that Yahweh's control of events is still very much alive in Israel's faith. It was true that he appeared utterly intransigent, but it was not thought of as vain to make appeal, for he might have mercy: 'Perhaps there is hope' (3.29*b*). In addition,

[1] Martin Noth, *Geschichte Israels* (Göttingen, 1950), p. 258.

Lamentations offers us some knowledge of the exilic ideals of prayer.

The nation begs Yahweh to behold its affliction (1.9*ef*), its reproach (1.11*ef*; 5.1), its rebellious exhaustion (1.20), the slaughter of children, youth and religious leaders (2.20). It pleads with the deity to give ear to the entreaty for help (3.56), to judge the cause of the innocent (3.59), and to restore the nation (5.22). The assumption is that Yahweh can do something about these conditions if he so wills. The most natural conclusion, granted the thought world of the ancient Near East, was the one Israel most stoutly resisted. Jerusalem did not fall because of Yahweh's impotence, but because of his strength. Since destruction is never final, affliction may be healed, reproach requited, rebellion forgiven, innocence justified, and the nation revived.

Lamentations makes it plain that appeals to all other quarters are fruitless. The passers-by do not respond with so much as a shred of mercy (1.12) but only add insult to injury by their revilings (2.15). The nations are oblivious to her pain (1.18). They boast in her downfall and make sport of her tragic lot (2.16). Healing from any human source is impossible (2.13). These categorical negations of earthly aid or comfort serve to intensify the urgent summons which the poet addresses to his people to call upon Yahweh (2.18, 19).

One word must be said about the intercessory prayer. 'Lift up your hands to him for your children's lives!' (2.19*ef*) adjures the poet. Thereupon the daughter of Zion, as the mother of all Israelites, pleads fervently for her children: the young, the priests and prophets, the aged, the maidens and warriors (2.20-22). One cannot help but think of the poignant picture of the ancestral mother Rachel weeping over her captive young (Jer. 31.15), and the later Jewish figure of the tribal ancestress in deep mourning for her offspring (Baruch 4.8-12; Syr. Bar. 10.16; 4th Esdras 10.7). The same sort of maternal pathos is encountered in the Babylonian mother goddess Ishtar who, after the great deluge, sang the funeral song over annihilated mankind. The fact that she is the goddess and not the nation personified is of course the important difference, but the same passionate intercessory concern is present, although there is no one to whom Ishtar may appeal for she herself has initiated the flood:

She bewails as one who has given birth:
　'The generation passed away has become loam
　　because I in the assembly of the gods commanded evil.
　Yea, I commanded evil in the assembly of the gods,
　　For the destruction of my people I commanded battle.
　I alone gave birth to my people!
　　And now they fill the sea like spawning fish.'[1]

A second instance of intercessory prayer is 3.49-51 where the poet in his grief vows to weep unceasingly until Yahweh looks down from heaven and beholds. There is the feeling that if he, as the bewailing poet, can be importunate enough he may gain the hearing of Yahweh who will then have mercy upon the whole city.

In his *magnum opus* on prayer, Heiler declares that lamentation is one of the prime ingredients of 'Prophetic' or 'Biblical' prayer and that it is quite in keeping with what he considers that type of prayer's essential content and motive: the unrestricted expression of compelling emotion, an involuntary and spontaneous discharge which the Old Testament figure 'outpouring of the heart' (cf. 2.19c) happily depicts.[2] In the Biblical complaint, anxious questions sometimes pass over into bitter reproach (Jer. 4.10; 15.9; 20.7; Hab. 1.2). Heiler cites Lam. 2.20 ff as an example of shockingly blasphemous lament.[3] 'Behold, O Yahweh, to whom thou hast done this!' is the audacious protest. Some construe this as a reference to the election faith of Israel. Overtones of that idea may be present, but a close study of the context would indicate that it applies to the mother and the priest and prophet. In other words, 'Lord, consider what you have done, turning women into cannibals and slaughtering your sacred ones in the holy place!'

We have, then, in Lamentations with its insistent appeals for Yahweh to intervene, that peculiar mark of Biblical prayer which naively seems to believe that God does not see atrocity or misfortune unless his special attention is called to it. Moreover there is the belief that importunity will bring results. Was Jesus scoring this attitude when he said 'they shall not be heard for their much

---

[1] Translated from the German rendering in H. Jahnow, *Das hebräische Leichenlied im Rahmen der Völkerdichtung. BZAW* 36 (1923), p. 177.
[2] Friedrich Heiler, *Das Gebet* (München, 1921), pp. 348-354.　　[3] *Ibid.*, p. 360.

speaking' (Matt. 6.7)? Or was he commending it when he urged that by her very importunity the widow was heard (Luke 18.1-8)? One has the feeling that by the boldest possible statement of the suffering, God will be moved to pity (2.20-22; 3.42-43) and thus the grim aspects of the book, the repetitions of sorrows and horrors are not solely for the catharsis of grief but are also intended to gain God's sympathy and aid. In truth, the chief characteristic of the prayers in Lamentations is that they are *motives* calculated to arouse God to action. Indeed this motivation of prayer as a means of *affecting* God survived and took on additional forms in later centuries.

Norman Johnson, in his study of prayer in inter-testamental Judaism, points out that the petitions to God were oftentimes accompanied by fasting, sexual abstinence, donning of sackcloth and ashes, beating of the breast and tearing of garments. These habits, ancient in origin, tended to become conventionalized, but they retained, nevertheless, the coloration of *motives*.[1]

> While many of these practices became a means of cultivating piety in the man himself, there can be little doubt that originally they were projected toward God's mercy and that the original function remained alongside the other.

Lamentations, with all its associated postures and gestures, offers a superb example of Biblical prayer in the starkest and most irreducible form. We see prayer in its naked objective power, passionately directed toward specific purposes. And if it is this aspect of prayer which is most baffling to the modern religious man, who would rather reduce prayer to a psychological act of piety, then it is precisely this aspect which our historical study needs to bring to the attention of Biblical theology as part of the data to which it must do justice even when that data runs counter to the mood of the day.

But what was there in the nature of God which prompted such violent prayer? Again we are thrust back upon the moral categories of sin and righteousness. That Yahweh had been perfectly justified in his harsh treatment of Zion is witnessed by the frequent confessions of sin. In the first and third poems, however, the

---

[4] Norman B. Johnson, *Prayer in the Apocrypha and Pseudepigrapha. A Study in the Jewish Concept of God.* JBL Monograph Series, Vol. 2, 1948, pp. 72 f.

author expressly enunciates the righteousness of God as a kind of fixed article of faith to which the doubting may cling. The daughter of Zion is made to say, 'Yahweh is righteous for I have rebelled against his word' (1.18*ab*). This is equivalent to saying, 'I have no excuse to offer.' In the middle poem, in what are the climactic verses of the whole composition, there is a magnificent utterance of the Lord's disavowal of all injustice:

To crush under foot all the prisoners of the earth,
To turn aside a man's right in the very presence of the Most High,
To mislead a man in his case, the Lord does not approve.

(3.34-36)

It is because of this assurance that the sorely tried nation is able to entrust its case to Yahweh, for he has contended for Israel's cause in days of old (3.58). He will judge the right of his people in the present crisis (3.59; 4.22). The foundations have been shaken but the divine government of the world is still administered from the steadfast throne of Yahweh. The easy optimism of the old enthronement hymns has vanished but their central affirmation still serves to express the faith of Israel: 'Thou, O Yahweh, dost endure forever, thy throne to generation on generation!' (5.19).

By means of this conviction about the enduring righteousness of Yahweh, his destructive demonic qualities were brought under control. Still, in sketching such a process, we must beware of thinking that for the Israelite this meant subjecting the deity to human definitions of the good.[1] As a matter of fact Yahweh

[1] This is the mistake that humanism and religious liberalism usually make. Because, in terms of the evolutionary process as a whole, the moral character of God was relatively late in rising to human consciousness, it is assumed that the discovery was simply an inference from the human situation. The fallacious deduction is to make of God a pious fiction or at best a useful ideal. The historical development of religion neither proves nor disproves the unchanging nature and purpose of God. It is altogether possible that religious man in his discovery of the moral nature of deity laid hold of something as objectively real as the natural sciences in their research into the laws of nature. Only the religious realm of discourse is competent to judge the issues involved. A good example of the approach of religious liberalism to the ethical monotheism of the Old Testament is in I. G. Matthews, *The Religious Pilgrimage of Israel* (New York, 1947), p. 126, where it is said regarding the writing prophets: 'That Yahweh was a moral being was one of their far-reaching contributions to religious thought. This was correlative to their interpretation that the leaders were doomed and that the existing institution violated human rights and dignity. Building on what to them was axiomatic, they concluded that Yahweh

remained self-determined but that self-determination revealed certain fixed points of fidelity and dependability. Because of his mystery and awe, his unassailability as God, there was no criticism of deity such as one finds so openly engaged in by the Greeks, who were able to dethrone the Olympian pantheon, analysing and dismissing them as one might treat any object of sensory perception. If we are speaking from the standpoint of Biblical revelation, the 'moralization of God' was not something which the Hebrews achieved, but something which God himself revealed. No matter what we think of this viewpoint ourselves, a faithful analysis of the mind of exilic Israel requires at this point that we forsake our philosophic and anthropocentric categories. To say this is not to undercut the importance of the historical context in which the righteousness of God was grasped; it is actually to affirm it, for, in Israel's faith, it is only through the medium of the collective historical experience of the covenant people that Yahweh makes himself known.

Rudolph Volz has observed that with the great writing prophets 'the demonic was separated from the holy'.[1] The sheer destructive power of Yahweh was in the service, not of rationally-stated moral norms, but of a righteousness which was holy. It was the great virtue of the category of the Holy that it could take on moral dimensions and still retain the primitive sense of mystery and 'shuddering'.[2] Two outstanding instances of this deepening of the doctrine of God by the interpenetration and fusion of the moral and the 'demonic' so that they become the Holy are found in Hos. 11.9 and Isa. 5.16:

was as fair-minded and as just as was man himself. In the world of men, where right was paramount, God himself must be the embodiment of right. This was a step forward in the realm of religious ideas.' Whatever measure of truth there may exist in this analysis, when Matthews talks exclusively of human rights and dignity, of inference and ideas, he betrays a wilful disregard of the prophetic frame of thought. An appraisal of this sort completely loses sight of the divine initiative and purpose which was the primary datum of the prophetic experience and message. Such interpretations easily reduce God from the rank of creator and controller of history to a phenomenon in the history of ideas. Can Biblical theology, i.e. theology which attempts to formulate the Hebrew-Christian faith, whether for historical or constructive purposes—can such theology deny the fundamental presupposition upon which the whole tradition rests?

[1] Rudolph Volz, *Das Dämonische in Jahwe*. Sammlung gemeinverständlicher Vorträge und Schriften aus dem Gebet der Theologie und Religionsgeschichte 110 (1924), p. 38.

[2] Cf. Rudolph Otto, *The Idea of the Holy* (London, 1950), esp. Chap. XIII.

I will not execute my fierce anger,
 I will not again destroy Ephraim;
for I am God and not man,
 the Holy One in your midst,
 and I will not come to destroy.

But the Lord of hosts is exalted in justice,
 and the Holy One shows himself holy in righteousness.

It is apparent that the Book of Lamentations perpetuates this insight, asserting it with all possible vehemence: Yahweh does not crush the captive, brush aside the clamour for justice, nor subvert a man in the rightness of his cause. We can readily understand how relevant this message was for the dark days of exilic despair. Israel is mistaken if she supposes that Yahweh has acted out of caprice or whimsey. Whatever the enormity and irrationality of the judgment from the human point of view, he has not disregarded the merits of the case. God is chastening Israel because he has her welfare at heart. He is guided by a righteous motive and a righteous goal.

Righteousness thus delineated borders on the covenant love of God.[1] Yahweh's *ḥesedh* appears triumphant over the miasmal bitterness and despair of the suffering prophet. It is the sufferer's remembrance of that covenant love which renews hope within him:

O remember my affliction and homelessness, the wormwood and the gall!
Thou wilt surely remember and bow down to me;
This I take to heart, therefore I have hope.
The covenant loyalties (חסדי, *ḥasdê*) of Yahweh that do not fail, his mercies (רחמיו, *raḥmāw*) that are not consumed,
Are new every morning; great is thy faithfulness!
'Yahweh is my inheritance!' says my soul, 'therefore I hope in him!' (3.19-24)

We are at once reminded of Zeph. 3.5:

The Lord within her [Jerusalem] is righteous,
 he does no wrong;

---

[1] Norman Snaith, *The Distinctive Ideas of the Old Testament* (London, 1945), p. 102 surveys the Old Testament usages of the term *ḥesedh* and concludes that, while it has definite associations with slowness to anger and mercy, its basic meaning is steadfastness and constancy

> every morning he shows forth his justice,
>   each dawn he does not fail;
>   but the unjust knows no shame.

Yahweh will not always afflict and reject, but will have mercy according to the abundance of his covenant loyalty. He does not arbitrarily or voluntarily mete out evil.

> For the Lord will not reject forever;
> If he grieves, he will have mercy according to the abundance
>   of his covenant loyalty;
> For he does not afflict from his heart, nor grieve the sons of
>   men. (3.31-33)

In contrast to his *ḥesedh*, Yahweh's affliction and rejection of men is temporary, the necessity in a given circumstance, but never the final word. He brings his anger to an end, but his covenant loyalties are never consumed and his mercies are never exhausted. The expression 'he does not afflict from the heart' is the high watermark in Lamentations' understanding of God. As long as such a view of God was held in Israel there was no danger of the extinction of Yahwism. The angry side of his nature, turned so unflinchingly against Jerusalem, is not the determinative factor in the divine purposes. Begrudgingly, regretfully, if there is no other way toward his higher purposes, he may unleash the forces of evil, but 'his heart' is not in it! His deepest and truest intentions are otherwise; they are bent toward *ḥesedh*. It is easy to see how a view of educational value in suffering could develop from such a faith.

Eichrodt singles out Lam. 3.22 ff as one instance of the strong relationship of the God of love to the sufferer.[1] The most outrageous blows of fortune and the severest chastisement cannot alienate the man who feels this attachment to his God. It is hardly necessary to remind ourselves that this attachment is not a matter of like attracting like, which is the moving spirit in all absorption mysticism and also in the magical religions of the Near East, among whom Israel's faith was an anomaly. The

[1] Walter Eichrodt, *Theologie des Alten Testaments* (Berlin, 1950), Vol. 1, p. 124. He regards Lam. 3 as an individual lament, but his insight applies just as well to a national interpretation. Attention is called to other examples from prayer literature, e.g. Job 33.16 ff; 36.15; Jonah 4.2; Sir. 4.17-19; Neh. 9.17, 31; II Chron. 30.9.

attachment which finds expression in the religion of Israel, beginning as early as Moses, is one which has been established by the prior initiative of God. Israel thus lays no claim upon God, but is claimed by him. This is the primal faith to which the prophets plead for a return. This is the faith of Lamentations. In the light of this fatherly connection, the Jews are to perceive God's grace within his judgment or, to state the matter more precisely, to recognize that his judgment was one aspect of his *ḥesedh*, even though it was not always possible to trace the direct connection between the two.

So intense had been the suffering that it was almost too much to expect that Yahweh would forgive. The poet does not come by his conviction of the divine love easily! Israel's sin had been very great (3.42) and Yahweh's anger pitiless (3.43). Köberle surely misunderstands the passage when he states that the line, 'We have sinned and rebelled; thou hast not forgiven' is proof that the people felt that God was obliged to forgive and therefore they are affronted.[1] But the very opposite is the case. If he does forgive, it will be a marvel of the goodness of God, for 'Why should a living man murmur, a man because of his sins?' (3.39). God, therefore, owes nothing to Israel, but from the ground of the divine mercy it could be hoped and prayed that he might turn his anger and be gracious. Still nothing is guaranteed or automatic, for it is not God's business to forgive, and Lamentations closes with the troubled question, 'Or hast thou utterly rejected us? Art thou exceedingly angry with us?' (5.22). Judging by the book as a whole, the poet was thoroughly disabused of Israel's claims upon God. He makes almost nothing of the doctrine of election (2.20*ab*?). Central to his thought, however, was Yahweh's faithfulness to his own nature and purposes which might once again result in favour to the chastised nation. We are left confronting the unfathomable divine love and mercy which can never be calculated but comes only as a gift. This is the sole comfort which the poet has to offer his people but it casts a ray of hope over the otherwise dismal scene.

The great power and incomprehensibility of God were two aspects of the divine nature that post-exilic Judaism seized upon.

---

[1] Justus Köberle, *Sünde und Gnade im religiösen Leben des Volkes Israel* (München, 1905), p. 368.

They were amplified and embellished in the great flood of literature from the sixth century on. Here, after all, was the only security and refuge for a people whose superficial optimism had been crushed by the adversities of historical life. We meet the omnipotent and veiled God in Ezekiel, Deutero-Isaiah, the P Code, and then again, with renewed emphasis, in Chronicles, Job, Daniel, and extra-canonical literature like Fourth Esdras. Rankin discusses with penetration the importance of the transcendent World-Creator to the post-exilic age and, in particular, notes its significance for the book last-named[1]:

> All that remains is faith in the Creator's will as being wise and good. This line of thought is taken up in Judaism at a much later date in the Fourth Book of Ezra when, after the destruction of Jerusalem by the Romans, the problem of suffering and of providence lay heavy on the heart of the stricken nation.

He fails to realize, however, that this very concern over providence was aroused by a similar historical situation six centuries earlier and that, in Lamentations, many of the interests and moods of the Wisdom literature are foreshadowed.

Of course it should not be overlooked that the conditions for the development of these ideas were long latent in the older prophets' stress on God's control of history. For example, Amos' chain of questions is a case in point (3.3-6). They may be understood as more than an effective rhetorical scheme for stating the law of cause and effect. His sense of the overpowering urgency of the divine will is clearly intended and there is more than an inkling of the later magnifying of Yahweh's majesty. But it remained for the exilic and post-exilic eras to exalt the omnipotence and inscrutability and to confess in dust and ashes that his ways were past finding out.

It is very noticeable in Lamentations that the ultimate appeal of the book is not alone to God's love and mercy but also to his unfathomed depths. Precisely as in Job, the very mystery of God is alluded to as at least a partial solution of the thorny problem of suffering:

[1] O. S. Rankin, *Israel's Wisdom Literature* (Edinburgh, 1936), p. 17.

Who is this who speaks and it is so, unless the Lord commands?
From the mouth of the Most High has there not gone forth evil
   and good?
Why should a living man murmur, a man because of his sins?
   (3.37-39)

The transcendence of God is seen in the appellation for the deity:
Most High (עליון, 'elyôn). It is circular reasoning to date the third
poem late because *Elyon* is a supposedly late title.[1] Actually a per-
usal of the other passages where it appears[2] indicates several which
are certainly exilic and some undoubtedly pre-exilic.[3] Furthermore, *Elyon* is a term used in Phoenician and Canaanite literature
which in most cases antedates the exile by centuries.[4] Even if
the usage of *Elyon* in Lamentations is the first in Hebrew literature,
it could not be imagined in a more likely circumstance and context. It is specious to shift the poem to a post-exilic date when all
its characteristics authenticate the historical situation of sixth-
century Palestine, simply because it uses a word that is not
common until a later time.

God as the author of evil as well as good was a familiar theme
in pre-exilic Israel (e.g. Ex. 4.21; 9.12; I Kings 22.23; Amos
3.6; Zeph. 3.6), but it did not become the subject of critical
reflection until Israel had tasted the bitter dregs of that evil.
Then the questionings were inevitable. Could this suffering, all
of it and in its every grim aspect, be the will of Yahweh? Thus
arose the first awareness of complexity within God himself—
levels of volition, if you will, which we often designate as per-
missive and primary will. Some distinction of the sort is presupposed when the same poet could say that 'he does not afflict

---

[1] Gustav Westphal, *Jahwes Wohnstätten nach den Anschauungen der alten Hebräer.*
BZAW 15 (1908), pp. 258, 262, gives the typical arguments for regarding *El Elyon*
as a late exilic development. He treats the significance of the name, especially in
the Balaam Oracles, and concludes that it was originally a Baal title, later applied
to Yahweh to express his transcendence over all other gods, and became frequent
in use when out of reverence the name of God was no longer spoken.

[2] Gen. 14.18-22; Num. 24.16; Deut. 32.8; Ps. 9.3; 18.14 cf. II Sam. 22.14; Ps.
21.8; 46.5; 50.14; 73.11; 77.11; 78.17; 83.19; 87.5; 91.1, 9; 92.2; 107.11; Isa. 14.14.

[3] A. R. Johnson, 'The Role of the King in the Jerusalem Cultus', *The Labyrinth*,
ed. by S. H. Hooke (London, 1935), pp. 81-85, contends that there was a pre-
Israelite Elyon cult at Jerusalem. If this is true then Elyon is an ancient title and
our post-exilic theories need drastic revision.

[4] Cf. citations in Köhler-Baumgartner, *Lexicon in Veteris Testamenti Libros*
(Leiden, 1948-1953), p. 708.

from the heart' and also that 'from the Most High come forth good and evil.'

With this insight Israel confessed that slowly she was learning the bitterest lesson of the religious life—that there is no simple one to one correspondence between man's hope and God's will. In this sense, Lamentations is the true teacher of later Judaism, even more so than the other more prominent exilic books, for its author was the first to acknowledge that his people's sufferings were dealt them by a God whose purposes are not always apparent and, therefore, must forever elude the definitions of even an elected people. Lamentations thus goes beyond Deuteronomy and is not far from the chastened spirit of the Talmud: 'It is not in our power', said R. Jannai, 'to explain either the prosperity of the wicked or the afflictions of the righteous.' [1]

It may be assumed that the frequent confession of sin in Lamentations presupposes repentance. The recovery of a right relationship with Yahweh involves not only the admission of 'guilt' (עָוֹן, ʿāwôn) but repentance, i.e., 'turning' (שׁוּב, šûbh). Israel has turned from Yahweh to sin and her contrition must now express itself in just as definite an act of the will—a turning back to Yahweh. Repentance implies an abrupt break with the offensive conduct or state of mind (cf. Ezek. 14.6; 21.23; Amos 5.14 f; Hosea 14.2; Josh. 24.23; Dan. 4.24).

Following the assurance of God's goodness and love, the nation summons itself, as it were, to return to Yahweh:

Let us search and examine our ways, and return to Yahweh!
Let us lift up our hearts not our hands, to God in the heavens!
We have sinned and rebelled; thou hast not forgiven. (3.40-42)

Such a 'return' to the Lord is more than a flight to consolation or a petulant play on the divine sympathy. It is accompanied by a searching and re-examination of the national ways (cf. Ps. 32.3, 5). Critical introspection gives way to the lifting of the heart to God and the confession of sin. There is the suggestion here that the poet is aware of the need for a new heart which was a

[1] *Pirke Aboth* iv. 19. Quoted in C. G. Montefiore, *Lectures on the Origin and Growth of Religion* (London, 1893, 2nd ed.), p. 451, who also remarks: 'No feelings rooted themselves more deeply in Judasim than those of absolute faith in God and unconditional resignation to his will.'

prophetic insight so superbly stated by Jeremiah (31.31-34). At any rate there is the realization that now the people have done all within their power. They wait penitently and contritely for the divine forgiveness.

Erich Dietrich has called attention to the fact that in the Old Testament, while repentance is often pictured as the work of men, it is also frequently described as the work of God. No contradiction was felt for 'we must herewith emphasize that the Old Testament in general has no systematic doctrine concerning efficient causation'.[1] He singles out the presence of both human and divine operations in certain of the prophets.[2]

It is noteworthy that just this coexistence of the human and divine aspects of repentance is seen in Lamentations. The closing exclamation of the book vehemently calls upon the Lord, 'Turn us to thyself, O Yahweh, and we shall be turned!' (5.21). This plea must be interpreted against the backdrop of the utter supineness and exhaustion of God's people so painfully pictured throughout the poem, a lingering abjectness born of wretched servitude and the despairing conditions of life, plus the great burden of sin and guilt that Israel bears. In herself she knows no power to return to Yahweh. But, while the regal vigour of Israel is destroyed (5.16), Yahweh dwells resplendent upon his throne of world government (5.19). The consequence that our poet draws is that if the Jews are to turn to Yahweh then he must initiate the process of returning.

In Lamentations 5.21, as in the Jeremiah parallel of 31.18, it is difficult to know whether it should be interpreted politically or spiritually.[3] Certainly it is not a matter of 'pure spirit'. The parallel hemistich, 'renew our days as of old!' sounds suspiciously like a return of the kingship, the temple, and the religious order (cf. 1.7). However there is something additional. In the first

---

[1] Erich Kurt Dietrich, *Die Umkehr (Bekehrung und Busse) im Alten Testament und im Judentum* (Stuttgart, 1936), p. 125.

[2] *Ibid.*, pp. 122-125, 149-152, 161-165. Cf. e.g. Zeph. 2.1-3 and 3.11-13; Jer. 3.12 f, 22; 4.14; 7.3, 5; 18.11; 25.2; 29.13; 35.15 and 15.9; 24.7; 31.18, 31 f; Ezek. 14.6; 18.21; 33.11 and 11.9 f; 36.25 ff; 37.23; and Isa. 46.12; 55.3 and 44.21 f.

[3] Erich Klamroth, *Die jüdischen Exulanten in Babylonien*. Beiträge zur Wissenschaft vom Alten Testament 10 (1912), p. 36, finds that the fifth poem was written in Babylon (cf. v. 2) and says that 5.21 is simply a thoughtless imitation of Jer. 31.18 and thus refers to a purely external restoration. It means simply, 'lead us back from exile to your land, to your residence upon Zion, in order that we may again build an independent nation.'

place, as Dietrich stresses, this prayer is uttered in Palestine and cannot be explained simply as a return of the exiles.[1] Furthermore if a restoration of political life were primary in the poet's mind, one might have expected the more suitable expression 'restore our fortunes' (שוב שבות, *šûbh šûbhôth*), cf. Deut. 30.3; Jer. 12.15; 30.18; 33.21; Ezek. 39.25) instead of 'turn us to thyself' (השיבנו אליך, *hašîbhēnû ēlêkhā*). Here is a clear parallel to 3.41, 'Let us lift up our hearts not our hands *to God*' (אל-אל, *el-ēl*). But it is this turning to God which Israel, because of the magnitude of her sin and suffering, is unable to accomplish. She has exhausted herself in frenzied prayer and to no effect. Although the modes of his working are not clear, if God were to turn Israel's heart to himself then a true restoration of her fortunes would occur. So there is a definite distinction to be drawn between 'turning to Yahweh' and 'return of fortune'. The one is the precondition of the other, i.e. conversion is required.

This notion becomes increasingly normative for post-exilic Jewish ideas of repentance. The heinousness of sin and the weakness of man were so keenly experienced that the great gulf between God and man had to be bridged by the divine initiative (cf. Zech. 5.5-11; Dan. 12.10). In later Judaism, the cry of Lam. 5.21 was incorporated in the Eighteen Benedictions.[2] In Lamentations, therefore, we find repentance not only as the basis of favour and restoration but also repentance as an act made possible by God, namely conversion.

The submissive spirit which the Book of Lamentations inculcates is another of the motifs that can best be understood in the wider Near Eastern context. To some extent the stress upon submission is related culturally to the loss of dynamic, the weariness which overcame the Semitic world from the Assyrian era onwards.[3] Albright remarks on several non-Israelite analogies to the submissiveness of the Suffering Servant in Deutero-Isaiah.[4] Valuable as this orientation may be, attention must also

---

[1] Dietrich, *op. cit.*, p. 127.

[2] *Ibid.*, pp. 126 f. This is the famous Shemoneh 'Esreh or Amidah, the principal supplicatory prayer of the Jewish liturgy, v. Elbogen, *Universal Jewish Encyclopedia*, Vol. IV, pp. 22-27 and A. Z. Idelsohn, *Jewish Liturgy and its Development* (New York, 1932), pp. 93-109.

[3] W. F. Albright, *From the Stone Age to Christianity* (Baltimore, 1946), p. 240 f and William C. Graham, *The Prophets and Israel's Culture* (Chicago, 1934), pp. 58 f.

[4] Albright, *op. cit.*, pp. 254 f.

be directed to the Hebrew prototypes for the meekness of the Servant. The Prophets Zephaniah (2.3, 10; 3.11 f) and Habakkuk (3.16) contain early examples of the new accent on humility and passivity. But in Lamentations we come upon the most outspoken appeals for submission to be found anywhere in the Old Testament:

> Yahweh is good to him who waits for him, to the person who seeks him;
>
> It is good that one should silently wait for the salvation of Yahweh;
>
> It is good for a man to bear a yoke in his youth.
>
> He sits alone and is silent since it has been laid upon him;
>
> He puts his mouth in the dust, perhaps there is hope;
>
> He gives his cheek to the smiter, he is sated with contempt.
> (3.25-30)

Especially striking is the admonition, 'Let him give his cheek to the smiter', for it is in sharp contrast to the reproach and vengeance which elsewhere receive such violent expression. In this passage there is an extinction or suppression of all pride and personal feeling, the stilling of every angry protest. Why this indifference, this almost Stoic forbearance and self-effacement? Because the suffering originates with the Lord and is ultimately an expression of his goodness, the sufferer must wait upon his action (3.25-27). In fact it is good that the yoke of suffering be borne patiently, for even in adversity Yahweh displays his goodness. In the utter dejection of the sufferer, when he lay spent and crushed in the dust, at precisely that moment the possibility of hope was still alive. The grief that Yahweh has dealt out is not wilful nor perpetual but a seasonal chastening and tempering that is bound to give way to his compassion and love (3.31-33).

At first glance this strikes us as quite different from the ordinary prophetic attitude. For example, Jeremiah railed bitterly at his enemies and was restive under their scorn. Yet the difference is not so great if it be remembered that submission in Lamentations is an admonition, an exemplary standard, and even within the same poem the old cry of vengeance is raised once more (3.66). But to say that submissiveness served as an exhortation is not to rob it of its meaning, for by means of his faith in Yahweh the poet was able to believe that even the smitings and insults of the foe were embraced in Yahweh's plans, and though only a pervert could delight in the mockery, the present pain could be endured.

The persistence of the submissive spirit as a motif in Hebrew literature is especially evident in Second Isaiah's characterization of the Servant of Yahweh (42.2-4; 49.4; 50.5-7; 53.7). It is easy to believe that this spirit of acquiescence in suffering, in order that God's good purposes might be achieved in his own time and way, was one of Second Isaiah's debts to the Book of Lamentations. The fact that the books were written in different lands, Lamentations in Palestine and Second Isaiah in Babylon, is no great difficulty. From the prophet Ezekiel it is clear that there was constant communication between the two areas.[1] That the pupil went beyond his mentor is indisputable. For one thing, the goal of exaltation and triumph is much more articulate in the Suffering Servant passages. There is an exuberance and abounding hope which would not have been natural for the dark hours in which our poet wrote. Yet it is conceivable that the patient spirit of Lamentations, plodding though it be, was the necessary prelude to the flights of the Babylonian prophet. It is Lamentations, and not Ezekiel or Deutero-Isaiah, which shows how the Jews bore the first dismal doubts and wild griefs and deep despair of their fate and by 'laying the spectres low one by one' were able to preserve their common faith in Yahweh so that at the propitious hour the prophet of a more certain hope might announce the New Creation.

Because in the suffering there was the promise of good, it is clear that the attitude enjoined was not simply passive meekness or a mere compliance with fate. There was some apprehension of the sufferer's participation in the greater good which endures beyond the city's rubble and the nation's fallen pride (3.25-27). It was, to be sure, a punishment for sin and should be accepted without murmur (3.39), but it was also man's part in the divine plan. H. H. Rowley in a comparative study of attitudes concerning submission in suffering as found in Hinduism, Buddhism, Confucianism, Islam, Judaism and Christianity, reports that in the

[1] Cf. Henry A. Redpath, *The Book of the Prophet Ezekiel* (London, 1907), p. xxxix, and Volkmar Herntrich, *Ezechielprobleme BZAW* 51 (1932), p. 129. Herntrich theorizes that, like Ezekiel, Lamentations was a Palestinian product which underwent later Babylonian revision.

Semitic religions, particularly Judaism and Christianity, the submissiveness is not prostration before an arbitrary destiny but
subservience to a greater good which the deity is bringing to
pass.[1] Suffering becomes creative and is 'received with an activity
of spirit, that seeks to learn its lessons and to appropriate its
profit, and not merely with resignation'.[2]

To what extent that spirit has permeated our book is another
question. It is not the constant thought which Jerusalem enter-
tains, for she is much more concerned with the bitterness of
suffering and the pangs of sin. Yet when there is pause for
reflection, some elements of hope and promise insistently emerge.
The restive mood of the laments shows that passivity is not the
total intent of the poet. His consciousness that the disciplinary
suffering is only temporary indicates that the waiting is not fruitless nor without expectation of better things. An intimation of
suffering that is purposeful is the central teaching of Lamentations,
the axis around which all the confessing and lamenting revolves.
The resulting submission and resignation became ever more
firmly entrenched in the ethos of Judaism (cf. e.g. Sir. 2.1-5;
the prose setting of the Book of Job; and in the Talmudic period:
Berakoth 5*a*, and *Cant. Rabba* II.16.2).

As a result of our close scrutiny of the religious message of the
Book of Lamentations we are compelled to assign it to the main
stream of Hebrew prophecy. Again and again we have discovered
points of essential agreement with the great prophetic teaching.
Some critics object that if it were truly in the prophetic tradition
the hope offered would be more positive in tone. For example,
C. J. Ball contends[3]:

> There is no trace of his [Jeremiah's] confident faith in the
> restoration of both Israel and Judah (Jer. 3.14-18; 23.3-8;
> 30-33) nor of his unique doctrine of the New Covenant (Jer.
> 31.31-34) as a ground of hope and consolation for Zion.

But it should be apparent that Ball, in his anxiety to dismiss
Jeremianic authorship, has failed to take into account the several
ways of expressing prophetic hope in the future, some quite

---

[1] H. H. Rowley, *Submission in Suffering* (Cardiff, 1951).
[2] *Ibid.*, p. 62.
[3] C. J. Ball, 'Lamentations', *Encyclopaedia Britannica*, 11th Ed., Vol. 15, p. 128.

different than those familiar to Jeremiah. If Lamentations deviates in certain respects from Jeremiah, it is no more than the difference between an Amos and a Hosea or an Isaiah and a Micah. Disinclination, or even actual disproof, of Jeremianic authorship must not be confused with the denial of prophetic affinities.

It is equally futile to make the hope innocuous by dating the third chapter after the restoration.[1] All attempts to minimize or deny the optimism of Lamentations are in danger of ignoring the peculiar vitality of Hebrew-Jewish faith which is strikingly evidenced, as H. W. Robinson remarks, in the fact that Israel's 'faith in Yahweh increased as her historical position decreased'.[2] It deserves reiteration that the Book of Lamentations displays precisely this baffling character: it originates in a period when Israel's historical life is in decline but it bears witness to a quality of faith which has been deepened by the catastrophe and, if anything, is in the ascendancy.

Briefly, how may we formulate the content of the hope which stirred in the mind of the author of Lamentations? It is not predicated on the prevailing conditions. There is nothing in the external situation (not even a Cyrus! cf. Isa. 44.28; 45.1-14) to offer the least bit of encouragement. In fact the ruined city and wasted countryside still stagger under the burdens of defeat. Attempts at economic, social, and religious reconstruction have been largely ineffectual (Chap. 5). So it is not surprising that the poet is unable to point to any instrumentality of hope in the contemporary scene. The ground of hope is in the unshakable nature of Yahweh's justice and love. His constancy guarantees that the disappointments and defeats are not ultimate inasmuch as sovereign grace stands behind and beyond them (3.36-39). As to the particular forms the future restoration would take, we may note the following:

1. There is the hope of universal judgment. The salutary factor in the book's treatment of vengeance, as we have seen, is the recognition that not Israel alone but all mankind must conform to the divine will (1.21-22; 3.34-36, 64; 4.21-22).

---

[1] Alex. R. Gordon, *The Poets of the Old Testament* (London, 1912), p. 77.
[2] H. Wheeler Robinson, *Inspiration and Revelation in the Old Testament* (Oxford, 1946), p. 142.

2. There is the hope of the satisfaction of guilt. The enormity of Zion's sin has raised the doubt as to whether forgiveness is possible (3.42; 5.22), but the close of the fourth poem states ecstatically that 'thy punishment, O daughter of Zion, is accomplished!' (4.22). And this statement is made in the same poem that so firmly emphasizes the unparalleled magnitude of the sin (4.6)! The fall of Jerusalem, the ruin and bloodshed, a fate worse than Sodom's, was accepted as the just but ample recompense of the guilt of Judah. The tremendous consolation which this oracular word must have brought is conveyed in the enthusiastic praise of the Midrash[1]:

> The Rabbis said: 'Better was the Book of Lamentations for Israel than the forty years during which Jeremiah inveighed against them.' Why? Because in it Israel received full settlement for their iniquities on the day of the Temple's destruction. That is what is written, 'the punishment of thine iniquity is accomplished, O daughter of Zion.'

Immediately we recall the comforting words that introduce the prophecies of Second Isaiah (40.1-2). The prophet has taken up the assuring word of Lamentations and added the significant detail of *double* punishment. After years of exile and suffering subsequent to the writing of the fourth chapter, it would be natural to assume that if restitution for past sin had been fully paid at that time, then an excess of atonement had surely accrued to Israel's favour by the time of Cyrus.

3. There is the hope of the end of exile. Those who remained in the land must have felt keenly the loss of Judah's leadership, especially after the brutal assassination of Gedaliah (Jer. 41). With several thousand of the choice citizens deported to Babylon, the Israel of God was actually a divided Israel until such a time as the exiles might return. In 4.22 the promise of their release is distinctly sounded with the words: לֹא יוֹסִיף לְהַגְלוֹתֵךְ *lō yôsîph lehaghlôthēkh*, which may be translated either 'he will never again carry you into exile' or 'he will keep you in exile no longer'. The sentiment is the same: the deep longing for a united Israel.

4. There is the hope of political and religious restoration. The content of the plea to 'renew our days as of old' (5.21) implies at

---

[1] A. Cohen, tr., *Midrash Rabbah. Lamentations* (London, 1939), pp. 234 f.

the very least a return of national freedom under king and priesthood with independence of movement, re-establishment of civil order and the exercise of worship and festivity.[1] All the sacred memories of a theocracy, of the favours and privileges of a select people, formed a halo around the past. It is too crass to call it political restoration alone, but it is too abstract and vapid to call it a spiritual restoration. Since Hebraism had so long been institutional, it was impossible to think of a bright future without the reconstruction of those ancient and venerated forms through which God made his will and goodness known. Lamentations thus foreshadows that compound of the devoutly spiritual and the rabidly institutional which formed the ethos of the New Israel (cf. e.g. Psalms and the Priestly Code).

Our delineation of the hope has remained rather indefinite at best. The passage which gives the most eloquent expression to that hope, namely 3.19-33, lacks any concrete account of its object, but it communicates to the sympathetic reader, better than a definition or a programme, the indestructible optimism of those who faced history with the secure faith that the future belonged to their God. With great sobriety and with earnest persuasion the Book of Lamentations proclaims Israel's incredible faith in a history creating and controlling God—a faith to which two of the solid facts of history still add their testimony: the survival of Judaism in the face of impossible odds and the rise of Christianity through which the boons of Israelite religion have been spread throughout the world.

[1] J. Pedersen, *Israel*, I-II, p. 488, shows that such a plea does not mean to turn back the progress of time but to bring again the substance of those days for 'the events with their character and substance make time alive'.

CHAPTER SIX

THE SIGNIFICANCE OF LAMENTATIONS

Our study has led us through many bypaths in an effort to grasp the total setting and message of the Book of Lamentations. We return now to the main road and consider, in retrospect, what we have learned concerning this much neglected document. What insight does it provide for Old Testament faith? What has it contributed to the shaping of Judaism? What is its permanent value for Christian faith?

I. *The Book of Lamentations is a superb illustration of the great lyric movement of the exile*

There can be no question about the literary excellence of these five poems. Among the collective laments of the ancient Near East they are without peer. Under the discipline of acrostic form and the chaste economy of the *Qinah* metre, the poet has created in clearly defined strophes a sincere and powerful vehicle of expression. His wealth of imagery is ceaseless; his turn of phrase generally felicitous. The old forms of speech are employed, but under the stress of emotion they are given unexpected depth or combined in original ways.

The question of the relation between the Psalter and other Biblical poetry is not easily answered, but there is reason to believe that the Book of Lamentations, written under the duress of the supreme historical tragedy of the Old Testament period, initiated fresh impulses in religious poetry. Certainly Ewald was right when he included Lamentations in his commentary on the Psalms,[1] and W. R. Smith was near the truth when he remarked[2]:

> Indeed the radical change of the religious life of the nation caused by the captivity could not fail to influence the psalmody of the sanctuary more than any other part of the worship: the Book of Lamentations marks an era of profound importance in the religious poetry of Israel, and no collection formed

[1] Heinrich Ewald, *Commentary on the Psalms* (London, 1881), Vol. 2.
[2] W. Robertson Smith, *The Old Testament in the Jewish Church* (London, 1892, 2nd ed. rev.), p. 218.

before those dirges were first sung could have been an adequate hymn-book of the Second Temple.

One finds in the laments of later Judaism no appreciable advance on the modes of expression set down in these exilic poems. As an embodiment of national sorrow, the literary imagery and even the terminology of lament remained determinative of later ages. In particular, the figure of Zion as a widow received its classic formulation in our book and was perpetuated in the Fourth Ezra, the Titus memorial coin showing Jerusalem as a desolate woman with the inscription, 'Judaea Capta', and the Pauline reference to the heavenly mother Jerusalem (Gal. 4.25 ff).

II. *The Book of Lamentations has had a considerable liturgical usage*

Composed for memorial recitation, the poems were employed regularly throughout the exile and perhaps thereafter on select occasions. Their phrases appear to have been familiar to the cultic-minded Chronicler (cf. II Chron. 36.16-19). But the most enduring liturgical use of the book has been in connection with the Jewish Ninth of Ab celebration. In orthodox Jewry it has been read in the synagogue since *c*. A.D. 70 to commemorate the fall of the city and the dispersion of Israel.

The Christian Church, oblivious to the pronounced sentiments of nationalism, has appropriated the book with special reference to the sufferings of Jesus Christ. Roman Catholic liturgy calls for the reading of passages from Lamentations on the last three days of Holy Week. Each of the lessons closes with the response and versicle, 'Jerusalem, Jerusalem, convertere ad Dominum Deum tuum'.[1] *The Book of Common Prayer*, with the exception of the Second Prayer Book of Edward VI, has regularly included passages from Lamentations for reading during Holy Week. Selections from the poems are also found in the *Book of Common Worship* of the Presbyterian Church U.S.A. as prescribed reading for Holy Week and other times in the church year.

Yet in the preaching ministry of the Church the book appears to have played an inconspicuous part. The writer cannot recall ever having heard a sermon based on a text from Lamentations and it is omitted from the educational materials of all denomina-

---

[1] Eduard Nägelsbach, *The Lamentations of Jeremiah* (New York, 1871), p. 2.

tions known to him. This is indeed unfortunate, for in our modern world where the reality of communal suffering is so great, the experience and message of Lamentations is extremely relevant.

III. *The Book of Lamentations is a forceful expression of the grief and despair of national disaster*

This is no perfunctory mimicking of sorrow but a deeply honest outpouring of grief over a communal tragedy which the poet has permitted himself to feel. He has participated vicariously in the multitudinous pains and griefs of the stricken populace and bound them all in a passionate outburst that ably avoids banality on the one hand and sentimentality on the other. He has expressed the overarching sorrow of alienation from his God.

> As the Hebrew lyric of joy attained its greatest heights only in the rapturous outpouring of the poet's soul to his God; the Hebrew song of mourning attained its greatest perfection, not in sorrow for the dead, but in anguish when the wrath of God was poured out upon the sin of His people.[1]

That this proves our poet to be neither a prophet nor the son of a prophet is to misunderstand the prophet altogether, especially the exilic prophet. Ezekiel's denunciations of his sinful people are among the most caustic and acrimonious in the Old Testament, but in the face of the changed situation of the exile he turned to pastoral ministration.[2] Deutero-Isaiah spared no effort to bolster the fainting spirits of his people. Why should not the poet prophet of Lamentations do the same? It is a sad caricature of the prophet to regard him as a man insensitive to the feelings and sufferings of the sinners he condemns (cf. even Amos' intercession in 7.2-4 and the reproof of Jonah's callousness).

IV. *The Book of Lamentations stands firmly in the great prophetic tradition of Israel*

Although on literary grounds it is highly doubtful, there is nothing in the book that Jeremiah could not have written (with the possible exception of his own eulogy in chapter three!), and its inclusion among the prophets in the Hellenistic canon and

---

[1] Henry T. Fowler, *A History of the Literature of Ancient Israel* (New York, 1912), p. 250.
[2] R. H. Pfeiffer, *Introduction to the Old Testament* (New York, 1941), pp. 542 f.

English versions was well advised. It possesses several features marking it indelibly as the work of one deeply influenced by prophetic conceptions.

A. *It is a vindication of the prophetic preaching of doom.* All five of the poems are pervaded with a sense of national guilt acknowledging responsibility for the catastrophe. They could only have been produced by a man who had taken to heart the prophets' messages. In the lyric beauty and passion of its phrases the sorrowing Jews found the perfect mode of expression, and subsequent ages have been the debtors of Lamentations' melancholy but just appraisal of the tragedy. One commentator, in estimating the tremendous influence of Lamentations upon the Jews, declares

> . . . it may not be too much to say that the sense of collective responsibility, the consciousness of communal guilt, so deeply rooted in the Jew, has received its strongest impetus from these mournful poems.[1]

B. *It counsels passivity toward the foe and toward God.* So clearly did the poet see in the enemy the instrument of Yahweh's judgment that he advised submission to the blows administered. Even when they were obviously an abuse of judgment, vengeance was left to the Lord. This attitude is not alone the result of Israel's historical limitation to action, but is in large measure a legacy of the preaching of Amos, Isaiah, and Jeremiah who believed that resignation to the foe and/or quiet trust in Yahweh was the only true course of action in the light of the divine control of history.

C. *It exhibits loyalty to Yahwism, firmly rejecting all temptations to syncretism.* That the prophetic response to the catastrophe was not inevitable may be seen in the attitude of those fleeing to Egypt who adopted the worship of the Queen of Heaven, inasmuch as for them Yahweh was defunct (Jer. 44). Second Isaiah's vigorous polemic against idols implies that many Jews were entranced with the worship of Babylon (cf. esp. Isa. 48.5). And the descriptions of Ezek. 8 and Isa. 57 show that throughout the sixth century foreign cults penetrated Judah and won numerous

---

[1] Israel Bettan, *The Five Scrolls* (Cincinnati, 1950), p. 78.

adherents among the Jews. From our familiarity with the colony at Elephantine, Egypt, we learn that strict prophetic standards of monotheism were compromised and eclectic forms of worship tolerated. When it would have been easy to turn to the lords of the conquerors or the nature cults of Canaan, Lamentations raised a consistent witness to the enduring faith in Yahweh shared by at least a substantial part of the exilic Jews.

D. *It shows that faith in Yahweh could exist independent of professional religious leadership.* In words as harsh as those of Isaiah or Micah or Jeremiah, Lamentations berates the faithless prophets and priests. Of course the failure of the prophetic vision and the priestly torah is lamented, but Yahweh has judged those who were false to their charges. The tragic fate of the religious leaders is their repudiation of God and not the result of divine weakness. Yahweh was still addressed for forgiveness and deliverance. This shows that the poet was aware of Yahweh as to a considerable degree independent of cultus and ecclesiastical structure.

E. *It preaches prophetic hope.* We have stressed that modern Biblical scholarship is becoming increasingly cognizant of the element of hope in the preaching of the great prophets of Israel. Furthermore, we have discovered that Lamentations echoes this conviction with confidence, placing in the sharpest juxtaposition the sin and punishment on the one hand, and the confession and hope on the other. The future of Israel is nothing apart from the future of God, and to the degree that God himself is mystery so Israel's future is mysterious. The readers of Lamentations were oriented toward the future as well as toward the past. That such hope did not come cheaply or glibly may be seen in the agonizing despair and doubt which are so frankly divulged throughout the book. Nevertheless, the promise of Yahweh, his *ḥesedh*, would triumph in the end.

V. *The Book of Lamentations was one of the major sources of Deutero-
and Trito-Isaiah*

Among the chief results of our study has been the discovery of parallels between Lamentations and Second and Third Isaiah, so numerous as to be hardly accidental. We have contended that the relative dates of the two documents make the direction of influence incontestable. Second Isaiah incorporated from Lamentations a large number of stylistic features and phraseology and even the structure and form of whole poems (cf. Isa. 47). Certain of the motifs and ideas of these later Isaianic passages are employed in such a way that they seem to presuppose the message of Lamentations. This is particularly true of the announcement of the satisfaction of guilt and the quiet submission of the Servant. The personalizing of national grief and suffering in Lam. 3 was one of the definite forerunners of the Suffering Servant conception. This means that among the many influences upon that exilic giant of faith who ranged over the whole of Israel's past traditions, room must be made for still another influence hitherto wholly ignored because of a fallacious system of dating that places the poems of Lamentations after the writing of Deutero-Isaiah. It is indicative of the intimate relationship between the two books that from at least the fifteenth century, on the Sabbath following the Ninth of Ab (the Sabbath of Comfort), the message of Isa. 40 was read in the synagogue.[1]

VI. *The Book of Lamentations represents a union of the priestly and prophetic aspects of Judaism*

As we have repeatedly observed, grief, confession of sin, and hope mingle in our book in a surprisingly free manner, creating a constant tension and vacillation between human weakness and helplessness and divine power and judgment. The poet was both a priest and prophet, if not in function, at least in spirit and purpose. The book is a notable example of the uncanny ability of the Hebrew-Jewish tradition to incorporate the prophetic religion within the forms of popular religion. This involved some compromise, but it also meant that religious faith could survive as a communal experience rather than as the exclusive possession of the occasional genius. It is doubtful if any of the prophets were categorically anti-institutional; it is certainly clear that whatever they intended, their witness has survived only because its revolutionary character worked like leaven within the institutional life of the Jewish community. Like Deuteronomy Lamentations is a studied attempt to state the burden of the

[1] Kaufmann Kohler, 'Ninth Day of Ab', *The Jewish Encyclopedia*, Vol. 1, p. 24.

prophetic message in a way applicable to the total life of a people.[1] Deuteronomy was publicly ratified as the law of the land; Lamentations was publicly recited as the manifesto of a people whose political destiny could no longer be self-determined. Deuteronomy did not stand at a sufficiently chaotic point in history, nor was its vision large enough, to recognize that historical life is full of incongruity. Lamentations accepts the Deuteronomic theory of judgment but senses an excess of punishment amounting to injustice. It admits the unknowable in human experience, but commends Israel to the hidden purposes of a just and loving God. It is possible to see in this fusion of prophetic faith and cultic recitation some confirmation of the existence in Israel of so-called cultic prophets.[2]

Finally, in one word, the special value of Lamentations for our day is that it offers an illustration of how to survive national calamity without falling into despair on the one side or self-righteousness on the other. It is first-rate literary evidence of the way in which Israel's faith in the one God and in its mission were preserved amid greatest peril. But the Book of Lamentations is of relevance in a modern world where the 'problem of captivity'

[1] This I maintain in spite of Gerhard von Rad's brilliant argument in *Studies in Deuteronomy* (London, 1950) to the effect that Deuteronomy originated from a priestly source to the virtual exclusion of creative prophetic influence. Von Rad does great service in calling attention to the priestly-cultic and national-martial spirit of Deuteronomy but his dismissal of prophecy as a more or less minor influence of the times is unconvincing. When he says that 'the prophetic in Deuteronomy is merely a form of expression, and a means of making the book's claim to be Mosaic real' (p. 69) he seems to sweep aside the solemn prophetic sanctions of social justice and the thunderous assertions of Yahweh's initiative which mark the book as prophetic, not to mention Deuteronomy's affinities with Hosea's life and death warfare with Baalism and foreign gods. Actually, with a more elastic conception of prophecy, i.e. one that does not insist that the prophet was absolutely iconoclastic and anti-institutional, it is easy to see how von Rad's view of the revival of amphictyonic patriarchal faith would be in harmony with the prophetic hopes. It need not be argued that prophets wrote Deuteronomy, but it seems indisputable that the author (or authors) thought the prophetic ideals so important that they should become the foundation of Israelite life. These authors share with the prophets not only common convictions about social justice but the fundamental platform that Israelite religion is a historical gift which Israel must constantly renew and, in a very real sense, constantly deserve. So, although it needs restatement, the older view of a prophetic-priestly compromise in Deuteronomy, accepted by a long line of Old Testament scholars (e.g. J. Wellhausen, A. Bertholet, K. Budde, B. Duhm, H. W. Robinson, J. Skinner, H. H. Rowley), is still not only tenable but absolutely compelling.

[2] Cf. esp. Alfred Haldar, *Associations of Cult Prophets Among the Ancient Semites* (Uppsala, 1945) and Aubrey R. Johnson, *The Cultic Prophet in Ancient Israel* (Cardiff, 1944).

(war, homelessness, hunger, brutality, eclipse of faith) remains a crucial problem. Can a nation accept its lot as in large measure a punishment for sin and then commit to the divine purpose those features of her fate which she cannot understand? And in so doing is ethical decision and historical activity undercut? Can this be accomplished without self-righteousness or the warping of history? Lamentations is the one Old Testament book that deals most pointedly with this problem. Its answer is practical rather than theoretical, issuing as it does from the vortex of suffering and temptation. From the Christian standpoint, its solution is partial and inadequate. But the Christian Church was soundly motivated when it embraced the Jewish canon. From the Old Testament we learn some things not made explicit in the New. Admitting its lack of any conception of vicarious suffering and its frequent vengeful spirit, the message of Lamentations is one which the modern church needs desperately to hear if Christendom is to understand its own mission as something more inclusive than the cultivation of personal piety while the common life of man perishes in the inferno.

INDEX OF BIBLICAL REFERENCES